My Journey From Southern Baptist to Talking to the Dead

Jill M. Jackson

Copyright © 2019
3 Graces Publishing
All rights reserved.
ISBN: 978-0-578-56075-5

DEDICATION

My heart is overflowing as I think of everyone who helped me become who I am today.

To my beautiful Mom, Gail. I honor you for the woman you are, and for teaching us that success and wisdom knows no gender. You showed us that women can embody the strength of an oak tree, and a spirit of an angel all at the same time. I miss you every day even though I know you walk with us. I love you more momma.

To my Dad, Buddy, thank you for the man you are and all you have taught me. My perseverance I owe to you. Thank you for loving me for who I am and offering your encouragement and support in everything I have ever done. I love and appreciate you more than you will ever know.

To my husband Daniel. Thank you for being my rock. Thank you for loving me so deeply with no boundaries and for holding space for me to birth my dreams. I love you to the depths of my being and look forward to us rocking our gypsy souls together until the end of time.

To my stepson Austin. Thank you for allowing me to be a Mom. I am so proud of the man you are, and it has been one of my great accomplishments helping to raise you. I love you son.

To my stepdaughter Haley. Although I didn't help raise you and we became family later in life, I'm very proud of you and love you very much.

To my sister Wendy. Thank you for being my sister and my friend. I'm so happy it was you walking this crazy road with me from so long ago. Thank you for always being there for me, day or night. I love you more.

To my editor, Jo Ann Langseth. Thank you for being an editor extraordinaire, while managing to keep the flavor of my message. This book would not be what it is without your amazing editing talents. I know the Universe put you in my path and I am sincerely grateful for you.

To William Kelly, who designed the book cover, thank you. The book cover is the first impression someone sees, and your intuitive skills in bringing mine to life are truly treasured. Thank you, my spiritual son, aka Michael!

And last but certainly not least, thank you to my Spirit Team, who always has my back. Thank you for lighting my path and guiding my way. I am truly blessed.

Table of Contents

Chapter 1

Southern Baptist

My name is Jill and I am a psychic medium. Welcome to my crazy world. This book is about my journey from the Southern Baptist Church to talking to the dead. They say the first step to healing is admitting the truth. It took me a very long time to grasp this concept. It would be many years before I would "come out of the psychic closet," so to speak. It took a great deal of courage to face the skeptics and nonbelievers and proclaim my gifts to the world.   I consciously began to see Spirits when I was about seven years old.   I'm certain I saw them before then; however, it's from this age that I have avid memories of spirits always being around me. When I was a child it frightened me, yet I thought everyone could see what I was seeing.

This is not something I talked about with my friends. Only one friend knew of my gifts. I tried my best to fit in and come across as normal and did a pretty good job of it. I was a cheerleader and on the dance team. I had a great group of friends and really enjoyed my young life. I'm sure some of the people I went to high school with are wondering why I didn't talk about seeing Spirits. As I said, I just assumed everyone could see them. And when I realized that everyone could not see them, I learned to put that aspect of me in a nice shiny box high up on a shelf for future use. Many of you may look back on your life and realize you made similar decisions and choices. Try your best not to chastise yourself if it took you years to realize your life purpose. I find that if we are true to ourselves in everything we strive to do, that is what matters most. For me, the times in my life when I was having the usual "normal" experiences and was not quite ready to "own" my gifts, led me to being who I am today.

One reason I am so passionate about helping other young people who have the gift of mediumship, or especially strong empathy, is that I know what a struggle it can be to make sense of it all at such a young age. I remember sitting out on my driveway, waiting for my parents to get home because I was frightened of all the Spirits showing themselves to me in my house. For instance, doors would open and close. Most children experience peer pressure and the myriad challenges of just being a kid. However, kids gifted in this way also have the challenge of knowing they are different. Many wonder why they were born with these gifts. I have since learned that mediums are portals through which Spirit flows; they are the beacons of light that helped open the portal in the first place. It wasn't until I was 12 years old and my grandmother passed away that I realized that everyone didn't see Spirits. My gran and I were super close. I loved her dearly. She had a childlike innocence to her that I adored. I fondly remember the nightly "toddy" she would enjoy. One of my favorite memories is of Gran and Papa teaching me all about football. Gran loved those Dallas Cowboys and she really loved Tom Landry. My sister and I stayed with Gran after school. I was heartbroken when she died. I will never forget the day she passed. She was only 52 years old. A few nights after her death, I was woken up in the middle of the night. My gran was floating above my bed! She was not sick anymore. In fact, she was radiant and smiling her beautiful smile. Telepathically she said, "I am doing wonderfully. I'm happy and I'm not sick anymore. I love you so much." I was elated -- over the moon happy that she had visited me! I ran to wake up my mom. Mom was already awake, and when I excitedly told her what I had just witnessed, she smiled and said, "Yes, Gran was just in here with me tonight too, telling me the same thing." Mom and I hugged and cried, but our tears were grateful tears, knowing that Gran had truly survived her physical body.

For the next few nights, I would awaken to the beautiful melody of Mom's jewelry box that played when the bottom drawer was opened. Mom would be sound asleep, and Gran would come into her room and open that bottom drawer so the music would play for us. When I heard the music, I would run to Mom's room and we would turn on the light to see the jewelry box's bottom drawer opened as far as you could open it! Gran really wanted us to know she was doing great and still around us!

I had no idea at the tender age of 12 that this experience with my beloved Gran would shape my life forever. Yet it did. It defined who I am. It would be many years before I was ready to accept the reality and the responsibility of my gifts. However, I can say this: After my Gran's full-form visitation in my room, I was never again afraid of the Spirits I saw. We all have those moments in our lives when a single event provides a significant thread that helps us weave together the tapestries of our life's masterpiece. For me, this was the first piece in the puzzle.

I want to take a moment to sincerely thank my beautiful grandmother for preparing me for my life's mission, as I know she is with my mom and smiling down on me as I write this book.

Before I delve into what it means to be a medium, it's important that I start at the beginning, to the early years that helped shape me into who I am today.

I was raised a Southern Baptist in the Deep South. The Bible Belt of Mississippi. In the Gallup poll of 2012, Mississippi was voted the most religious state in the country!

Are you starting to get the picture of why my story is more unique than most? And why I moved away as fast as I could?

As a child, I attended Sunday school and church every Sunday, and was proud of what it meant to be a child of God and a person of deep faith. As I grew older, however, questions began to form in my mind about what I was being taught. There seemed to be a dichotomy of messages being delivered from the pulpit. On the one hand, the pastor proclaimed that our Lord Almighty God is a loving God who loves each of us unconditionally, and if we declare that we are sinners and ask for forgiveness, all is well. Unless, of course, you are homosexual, or you don't buy into the exact story of Jesus as it's told in the Bible. Then, apparently, our loving Father sends you straight to a fiery inferno, where you burn for eternity.

Wow! This did not make sense to my psyche. How could God be so loving and pure, yet so mean at the same time? One of the benefits of being a psychic medium is having deep knowing's when something does not resonate as the truth. As I grew older, I began to have more of those deep and firm convictions whenever something did not make sense. I began to have increased difficulty reconciling what I had been taught from organized religion with what I knew to be my truth.

According to most religious authorities, our unconditionally loving God doesn't like homosexuals. It is written in Leviticus 20:13, "If a man lies with a male as with a woman, both of them have committed an abomination; they shall surely be put to death; their blood is upon them." This does not seem like something a loving God would "convey" to the men writing the Bible. What many people don't understand is that common ordinary men wrote the Bible. These scribes deciphered the information they believed to be coming to them from God. The God I know would not channel information to someone about murdering a person based on their inborn sexual preference. Another thing I find quite interesting is that the Christian religion preaches that psychics, mediums, and channels are evil and of the devil, yet they expect you to believe unquestionably that God channeled the information to the authors of each Book of the Bible. Things that make you go hmmm. But I digress.

Another red flag moment for me and religion was when I found out that our married pastor was caught having an affair with a married member of the choir. This was quite a shock to me, as I knew the pastor's wife and she seemed so lovely and trusting of her husband. I have often wondered how our pastor could stand up in front of the congregation preaching about the sins of infidelity and adultery while secretly meeting up later on with his mistress? This was my first exposure to hypocrisy in religion.

My husband has a similar story from his childhood church, relayed by his grandmother about one of their preachers. The married preacher was having an affair with the married organist. The preacher's wife found out about it and painted the door to the church red one Saturday night. When the church members showed up Sunday morning, they learned why the preacher's wife had painted the door red. This created a divide in the church. Yet some of the parishioners actually followed this hypocritical preacher to his next church! Again, something that makes you go hmmmmm. Organized religion has brought me many of those "cock your head to the side, eyebrow raised" moments.

After college, I moved to Orlando, Florida, where I decided once again to give organized religion a try. As I arrived at the church, I saw the preacher pulling up in his brand-new Mercedes-Benz. This made me uncomfortable as I knew there were homeless and hungry kids not only where I lived, but in other nearby areas. As I was standing in the newcomers' greeting line to meet the pastor, I tried to release any preconceived notions I may have had. When it was my turn to shake hands with him, he squeezed my hand tightly and winked at me. Flirtatiously, he told me he was very happy I would be a member of his church. I almost fell over backwards! I thought back to my original preacher having an affair while delivering his sanctimonious sermons each Sunday. I drove away that day shaking my head in wonderment about how so many people eagerly hung on these pastors' every word, never once questioning his or her behavior or ethics. This would be the last time I sat in a Baptist church other than when attending weddings and funerals.

Even though my experience with organized religion did not continue, I was very grateful that my mom had shared the concept of faith with me. I was taught to have receptivity and a belief in a Higher Being, a Creator, and this has served me well throughout life. I believe that our children should be introduced to the idea of God the Creator, Divine Source, or whatever term most resonates with each person. This opens them to the possibility and promise of faith in something far greater than themselves. This ineffable "something" may be seen as wholly pure, a great White Light, a loving Father-Mother, upon whom one may always lean. Such faith is something to aspire to, as this is our great privilege on Planet Earth. We are here to seek perfection, through many life lessons, which may allow our physical bodies to vibrate at an ever-higher frequency as we ascend toward God.

In recent years, many people have been turning from religion to spirituality. Let's look at why this is so. There are many different beliefs as to when religion began. Some historians claim it dates back over 40,000 years. According to many religious scholars, the first major religion was Hinduism. Judaism has been around for over 4,000 years, and Christianity a little over 2,000 years.

As I have researched each of these religions, I find a dominant thread woven throughout a common message. This message is one of fear. When you begin to study consciousness and expanding your own consciousness, the subject of vibration arises. Vibration and frequency are measured on a scale from low to high. The higher your personal vibrational frequency, the closer you are to Source or God. Everything is made up of energy. Quantum physics has proven this to be true. Everything -- whether it be an inanimate object, a plant, an animal, or a human being – is vibrating. Everything connects to everything else at a subatomic level. We are all intimately interconnected!

A wonderful book, *Power vs. Force*, by Dr. David R. Hawkins, explains the concept of "Vibrational Hierarchy." If all energy can be measured, we can then reason that all thoughts, beliefs, and words create an energy signature, so to speak. Thoughts and feelings such as anger, guilt, shame, envy, and fear vibrate at the lower end of the frequency spectrum. Feelings and concepts such as peace, love, joy, and acceptance vibrate at the higher end of the spectrum. Even if you are not a metaphysician or scientist, you can see the truth in this for yourself! Have you ever been around someone who is always a Negative Nellie? They worry about everything and/or tend to be angry at the world. How do you feel when you are around this type of person? More than likely you feel drained, sad, and depressed! This is because their energy sends out frequency waves that actually "zap" you when you are around them! On the other hand, I'm sure you know people who are almost always positive, filled with love and joy, and tend to see the cup as half full. People tend to be drawn to this type of person like bees to honey. They want to drink from the nectar of energy in their auric field.

I highly recommend reading books about energy and vibration. *Power vs. Force* is mentioned above. *The Seat of the Soul*, by Gary Zukav is also a great book. *The Honeymoon Effect: The Science of Creating Heaven on Earth*, by Dr. Bruce Lipton, is another must-read. I cannot stress enough the potential of setting an intention every day to raise your personal vibration. When you get out of bed each morning, take a few moments to express gratitude for the things in your life you are grateful for. This sets the bar for your personal vibration to be higher. Let's all do our part in creating a kind of domino effect from raising our personal vibrational frequency, which in turn raises the frequency of those we encounter, as well as Mother Earth.

Organized religion was born thousands of years ago, with the fundamental purpose of alleviating the fear of death. Slavish obedience by followers of its doctrines also ensured control of the masses by all-powerful clergymen. Of course, it goes without saying that there are organized religious institutions that don't manipulate using fear. This just happens to be the basis of many religions: using fear to control. When we consistently put ourselves in the energy of fear, this lowers our vibrational frequency, dulling our spirit and weakening our body.

We cannot discuss organized religion without examining the monetary aspect of it. The fraud connected to churches has been widespread in recent years.

There are two separate incidents that come to my memory about the church and money. The first is from when I was still a CPA and one of my tax clients came to me asking for copies of their last three years of tax returns. As I was getting them ready for her, I casually asked if she was trying to qualify for a new home. No, she said. "I'm trying to get accepted into a church I want to start attending." I stopped cold and asked, "Is this a joke"? "Not at all!" she assured me. "They just want to make sure you are substantially sound in the financial sense before accepting you." I was dumbfounded. How could this be? And how could people get on board with something so sinister?

Another example was one of my celebrity clients when I was a CPA/business manager. I will detail this period of my life in a later chapter; however, for this part of the story please understand that part of my job as a business manager was to manage the celebrities' money for them. I was a signer on all bank accounts. Per instruction from my client, I was to automatically deduct 10% from every check that she was paid and mail it to her church. I can tell you that this was a substantial amount of money! When her career began to wind down and it was clear her television show was not going to be renewed, I had a meeting with her to go over a strategy for managing her remaining wealth so that there would be enough to carry her through the rest of her life. I explained to her that we would need to stop mailing in those substantial checks to the church. She reluctantly agreed. However, when her series was finally cancelled, she blamed *me*, stating that God was not happy that she had stopped tithing, and therefore her series had been cancelled. I was shocked that she would blame me! OK, I know I'm a medium and that my life is full of bizarre phenomena, but was I in an alternate universe here? Where do I begin? First, in my view, God has better things to do than sit around and decide which TV shows are going to be renewed or cancelled. Secondly, this line of reasoning portrays a petty God who bestows good fortune exclusively on people of wealth and abundance who give churches large sums of money.

Putting aside my shock, I decided to come up with a plan to help my client. As her financial situation grew bleaker, I told her to go to the church for assistance. I reminded her that she had always described a loving church to me, one that constantly helps its parishioners. Excited about this idea, she proceeded to meet with the leader of her church. He told her that he would need to meet with a special committee for approval to help her. When he finally delivered the verdict that they were unable to offer monetary assistance, I thought this would be the moment she would wake up and leave the church. Instead, she vehemently defended their decision. However, as a silver lining to this story, they did offer her some undented canned goods.

I'm thinking back now to a woman who came to my Spiritual Center with a friend. Having recently lost her mom, she had a deep urge to consult with a medium. She was nervous even having a conversation with me. Finally, she explained that she had consulted with her preacher and told him she felt the need to have a session with a medium. The preacher then told her, "You need to grasp the fact that your mother is dead, and you will not see her or speak to her again until Jesus comes back." This harsh prediction shook the woman to her core. She cried as she relayed her conversation with this "man of God." Someone please explain to me how he is portrayed as the "good" one and I am portrayed as the "evil" one? I can tell you this: people who consult with me leave knowing that what this preacher told her is a blatant lie or, at best, a sad misconception. Our loved ones do survive the demise of their physical bodies, and their souls do continue on in another plane of existence. They are around us often and leave us many signs of this. It brings them tremendous joy to know that we know they are around us.

Another very religious woman came into our Center. She began looking around at our items for sale with disdain. She then told my husband that our "Middle Eastern" goods were making her very uncomfortable, because she loved Jesus. Daniel didn't miss a beat when he said, "Isn't Jesus from the Middle East? Then that makes us closer to Jesus!" Indignantly, she replied, "What exactly are you pushing here?" To which my clever husband replied, "Nonjudgement."

As of 2018, the Catholic Church had paid four billion dollars to victims of abuse by members of its clergy. Yes, you read that correctly. Billion. Can you begin to imagine what we could do with four billion dollars to help fight hunger in our world? In 2019, a Gallup Poll showed thirty-seven percent of Catholics agreeing that "recent news about sexual abuse of young people by priests" has them personally questioning whether to remain Catholic. In 2002, this number was only 22 percent. More people are leaving the Catholic religion than any other religion. The wealth of the Vatican is estimated to be around 15 billion dollars, and there's no way of knowing the cumulative value of the Church's real estate holdings. Jesus rode into town on a donkey. I personally think something has gotten lost in translation over the years.

It is not my intention to single out only the Catholics and the Baptists. I am simply pointing out the myriad of reasons why I made the personal decision to leave organized religion behind. It is my prediction that by 2025, around half of the US population will consider themselves more spiritual than religious. I realize this is a bold prophecy and I may be off a little on the timing, but I do see this unfolding. I believe the business of religion is a dying industry.

I can't tell you how many people have come to me for a reading and asked me beforehand if they are going to hell if they have a reading with me. This fear is especially noticeable since I have been back in the Bible Belt. I may shock a few readers when I assert: there is no hell. Please stay with me here. How can an all-loving God forgive us our sins while we are still in the physical world, yet if we happen to pass away without accepting Jesus Christ as our Lord and Savior, He will send us to a fiery hell for eternity? What happens to the people of the world who are not aware of who Jesus was? I can guarantee that there are some men and women living in the deep jungles who have never even heard of Jesus Christ. Are they doomed to burn in hell?

Some also preach that if you do not repent of your sins, you will surely burn in hell. Let's pretend that one of the preachers who has committed adultery repented and asked for forgiveness and all was well. The doors to the Kingdom of Heaven were open to him once more. But then one day he was tempted to sin again and found himself in bed with his mistress, who was also married. The poor sap had a heart attack and "died in the saddle". He did not have time to repent or ask for forgiveness before he died. Do you really believe that our loving God would send him to hell to burn forever? His wife may have wanted to buy him an express ticket there after finding out how he died, but the God I love doesn't behave this way. Ya'll, I have talked to a lot of dead people. (They are not really dead; they have just transitioned out of the physical body.) And many of the dead people I have spoken to were sinners who did not repent. Or they never asked to be saved or chose not to attend the new church on the corner to avoid tithing their 10%. And they are not burning in a fiery hell!

The God I believe in loves all of us. He does not judge us. His love is unconditional. Does this mean we can behave any way we choose? Yes, actually it does. We do have free will. Just don't forget about that pesky little thing called karma! The fact is, most of our souls crave raising our vibration by thinking good thoughts, speaking kind words, and doing good deeds. I have embraced a mantra to live by that truly encompasses everything – The Golden Rule. Do unto others as you would have them do unto you. Simple.

I enjoy debating ridiculous claims about psychic mediums that are being directed at me and other mediums by organized religion. One of their favorite Bible verses to use is Leviticus 19:31, which reads "Do not turn to mediums or consult spiritists, or you will be defiled by them; I am the LORD your God." Where do I begin here? Who wrote the book of Leviticus? I certainly don't claim to be a religious scholar, but I did do a little research and it is alleged that Leviticus is a record of a conversation (or series of conversations) between Moses and God. Most Bible scholars believe that the author was Moses. Moses was known as a prophet. If you could see me right now, you would see me shaking my head in an exaggerated fashion. Let me try to grasp this. It's not only okay that Moses was known as a prophet, it is celebrated that God spoke directly to him. Yet when I or other psychics claim we have received prophecies, religion tells us we are evil?

Moses claimed to have parted the Red Sea. Religious people read this claim and wholeheartedly believe that it happened. Yet when I claim that a deceased person appeared in my room to chat with me, I am considered a lunatic at best, or plain evil, at worst. Things that make you go hmmmmm.

Jesus himself was a medium. It is written in the Bible that Jesus spoke to Moses and Elijah, who happened to be dead at the time Jesus was talking to them. Christians may say, well, Jesus' gift was from God. Drum roll please! Mine is too.

My favorite part of this debate, I learned from my dad. When a fundamentalist Christian tries to tell me the Bible says I'm evil because I'm a medium, I love asking them if they are proud to follow the Bible and its teachings. They always exclaim, "Of course!" My friends, I'm going to cite some Bible verses that most of your fellow churchgoers are probably *not* following.

Leviticus 25:44-46 – "However, you may purchase male or female slaves from among the foreigners who live among you. You may also purchase the children of such resident foreigners, including those who have been born in your land. You may treat them as your property, passing them on to your children as a permanent inheritance. You may treat your slaves like this, but the people of Israel, your relatives, must never be treated this way." I may not be a religious academic, but I do know that God does not condone slavery of any kind! This verse is giving readers permission to purchase slaves as long as they are foreigners. I know for a fact my God did not channel this information to anyone.

Mark 12:19 – "Master, Moses wrote unto us, If a man's brother dies, and leaves his wife behind him, and leaves no children, that his brother should take his wife, and raise up seed unto his brother." How kind of Moses to think of a dying brother who has no children. And he's even kinder for asking the widow to take one for the team.

Genesis 19:8 – "Look, I have two daughters who have never slept with a man. Let me bring them out to you, and you can do what you like with them. But don't do anything to these men, for they have come under the protection of my roof." I can't even bring myself to discuss this one. And some want to assert that I am evil because of my gifts?

My harsh words may make it seem like I dislike Christians. This could not be further from the truth. What I have an aversion to are hypocritical fanatical Christians who want to throw stones at me and make someone shake in fear for simply wanting to communicate with their deceased child through me. Someone who wants to judge me. I feel the need to include one final biblical injunction: Matthew 7:1 – "Do not judge or you too shall be judged." Point made.

When I made the intentional decision to leave organized religion behind me, it felt very empowering. Looking back on my life, it was one of those moments when I stepped into my truth, refusing to participate in a system of control any longer. I realized that I am privileged to not only have a direct link to our loved ones, but that we each have a direct link to God as well! I choose not to get dressed up every Sunday and go sit in a building, listening to a sermon. Rather, I choose to view the beauty of nature as my church. I choose to listen to the songs of birds as my choir. And I will gladly listen to a message from my Spirit Guides any day of the week!

My Creator, the loving vibrating energy of Source, does not operate from a place of fear. The Divine Consciousness that I know as my God relates only to unconditional love and light.

And he loves us regardless of our religion or lack thereof.

Chapter 2
Being a Psychic Medium

There are a few professions that people find a bit odd to be practicing. Proctologist, mortician, and coroner are a few that come to mind. And oh yeah -- psychic medium. There are normally only two reactions I get from people who find out what my profession is. In the first scenario, the person is filled with awe and exclaims how cool it is that I can speak to the dead. The second and not so pleasant reaction is one of fear, and immediate recoil from me, as if I were a member of a satanic cult or something. One would think that I walk around carrying "evil stardust" to toss on them. Or that I instantly know all their deep dark secrets. Obviously, neither is true. Human Jill now frankly reminds herself that over the years, there were some people she would have gladly doused with this imaginal dust. And not the good kind of magic stardust, either.

Just because some of us have the gift of communicating with the other side doesn't mean we are like Barbara Eden in *I Dream of Jeannie*, where we can snap our fingers or blink, and someone disappears or freezes like a statue! You will notice as you read my story that I sometimes refer to myself as Human Jill. We are souls, having a human experience. I try my best to stay as pure and loving as possible. But hell, sometimes I have strong human reactions to things. Like when someone harms an innocent animal. My angel wings retract, and my Human Jill jumps into action. We must all remember that we did choose a human 3-D lifetime to experience. And we do the best we can do.

Most of us do not choose to be a psychic medium. Trust me, it's not the easiest path to navigate. As a medium, you rarely *feel* normal. Many times, we experience a profound sense of loneliness in our lives. We feel misunderstood and judged. The pressure is always on to help heal others, ease their pain and sorrow, and help them grow along their path. Pressure is also always there to answer friends' questions while in "psychic mode." Whether it is true or not, we psychics feel that when a friend or family member asks us a question, they are expecting us to answer with our psychic hats on. They may not have this expectation at all, or perhaps only some of the time, but it is a weight that permeates our psyche.

Wealthy people often wonder if someone is their friend because they are loved and adored for who they are, or because they have money. Most psychics feel the same way. Is someone our friend because they truly love and appreciate who we are as humans, or are they our friends because much of what we say comes from a place of otherworldly interdimensional wisdom? I have ended friendships that were out of balance because as much as I loved the friend, the truth and reality of the situation was, they were mainly my friend because I always gave great advice. They were not there for me when I needed them. There must be balance in everything. An ebb and flow. A sacred dance. You may be wondering how I don't recognize this trait in someone immediately if I am such a great Psychic? My Mom used to ask me the same thing! As Psychics, we all have certain "gifts" that work well for us. We each have a Psychic Toolbox of sorts and we learn over the years which tools work best for us, as every Psychic is different. This just happens to be a tool I am missing in my box! I always think everyone is pure and has good intentions.

Some of my psychic colleagues have shared the same story with me of how they ended friendships when the realization suddenly hit that their friend was using them as a free psychic. Friends, this is painful! The wealthy person who realizes that their friend is in it for the perks and not because they value the friendship must feel the same pain.

My psychic medium friend and colleague Sally Rice and I have shared a few laughs over this. She recalled a so-called friend emailing her and asking, "Can you please just quickly look into this one matter for me?" The problem was that it was the fifth "quick" question she had requested. Our stance as professional psychics must be one of solid boundaries. Sure, we will be happy to look at your quick question. Schedule a session and we will connect for you. That may seem cold or cruel. But let's think about this and put it in proper perspective. You don't ask your dog groomer friend to give your dog a quick summer cut at the neighborhood cookout. Nor do you ask your dental hygienist friend to quickly floss your teeth for you while you are waiting for a movie to begin. Guys, please respect our boundaries too! We have only so much battery power to plug into on any given day, and we need to conserve that for our clients, who have properly scheduled a session with us.

Yes, being a psychic medium can be a lonely road to travel. I have had someone pick up her yoga mat and move away from me across the studio when she found out I was a medium. We mediums know we are not "normal." We often know things before they happen. Many times, when a friend who is not psychic is telling us a story, we are shown exactly how it ends or what they should do about it. The problem is that the person may not want to hear what we have to say. There are times when our spouses are discussing a situation and we know immediately how things should be handled. We don't know how we know. We *just know*. Some people view us as know-it-alls. And not in a good way! Human Jill has had to learn the hard way that her husband desires to be his own individual person and experience his own life lessons and negative experiences —even if some of those bad experiences could have been avoided if he had just listened to his psychic wife! Of course, this works both ways, since I have a psychic husband! I will discuss this further along in the book.

Another time we feel like we have three heads is when we are trying to be normal at a party or gathering. For example, people tend to talk about their normal lives of job problems and their kids' sports and whether they should add on that room addition. It's hardly a great time to talk about the Spirit that woke you up the night before …or how your ears have been ringing really loudly, which alerts you to the fact that there will be a very large earthquake in a few days. And there is not a damned thing you can do to stop the quake. Generally, people don't want to think about such things when they're trying to relax over a few beers! Imagine, if you will, this conversation. Bill asks Mary to grab him another beer as they are excitedly describing how well little Tom did the day before on the ballfield. They then turn and ask you how your day has been. Me: "Well, my ear tones have been deafening and there was nausea with it this time, so this means we will be having a 6.5 earthquake, and there will be a tsunami along with it." Dead silence as everyone stares at you as if you are an alien with the green face and all! These are the kind of topics we psychics and mediums discuss among ourselves, though. I'm not saying we don't at least attempt to live normal lives. And many mediums do have kids and go to sporting and school events but trust me -- we rarely discuss what *really* goes on in our daily lives! My psychic medium friend Leanna Marino will text me when the vertigo, nausea, and ear tones hit her because nine times out of ten they are disabling me as well. We are both Mother Earth Sensitives. This means we have such a connection and resonance with Gaia that when She is in distress, we *feel* it in our physical bodies. A few days before the deadly earthquake and tsunami of 2004 hit, I was nearly bedridden with extreme vertigo, ear tones and ringing, and instead of the "normal" nausea, I was vomiting.

And yes, Spirits do follow us around. Not 100% of the time, but a lot. For me personally, when I am enjoying a service which involves the person touching me, such as a massage or a pedicure, it is more difficult to keep the boundaries and barriers up. Through my years of study with some of the most experienced mediums of our time, I have learned to shield and keep proper boundaries up. In turn, this is something I teach my students. Connecting to the Spirit World takes a lot of our energy. Think of it as a battery, and the battery has only so much charge or energy on a given day.

If a medium doesn't learn to keep their battery on "rest mode," he or she will be completely drained by the end of the day. But for some reason, when someone is touching me, those shields come down a bit. When I am trying to enjoy a massage and the massage therapists loved one is begging me to relay a message, it can be frustrating! After all, it is important for mediums to recharge and take care of themselves. That pampering session is supposed to be "Me Time!" This seems to be one area that sensitive people find challenging: to be the recipient of receiving. We are always giving to others. It is extremely important for psychics and mediums to practice self-care, or their battery life, so to speak, will certainly be shortened.

I recall a time I was attempting to enjoy a pedicure. The pedicurist's grandmother would not leave me alone! I begged her to allow me the few moments of relaxation. She was not having it. She even tried to guilt me into giving her granddaughter the message! Finally, I agreed. The next hurdle was the fact that her granddaughter did not speak very much English. So, I asked her colleague if she would translate for me while I translated for the Spirit World. I did ask permission first from the granddaughter. This is a pet peeve of mine and something I teach my mediumship students. It is not okay to read someone without their approval. My psychic friend and colleague Duann Kier humorously calls this a "drive-by psychic shooting!" I was able to deliver the message from the grandmother in spirit to my pedicurist. This particular grandmother was one of the pushier ones. The majority of loved ones will respect our boundaries if we ask them to. This is another misconception about the Spirit World. Most people think that when our loved ones go to heaven or the Other World, they instantly become angels. Not true! I have found that if someone was loud and pushy in the flesh, they are probably going to be loud and pushy on the Other Side!

Another time the barriers try to come down for mediums is when we drink. Even a single glass of wine or a cocktail will start threatening those barriers. I must constantly place extra layers of protection around me when I am in a bar listening to music. I remember one occasion when I was in a favorite wine bar enjoying an awesome band when a Spirit Communicator started talking to me. He was very upset with someone at the bar. Apparently, this Spirit Communicator, named Joe, had left with this man one night after partying and had been intimate with him. Joe had feelings for this guy, but had been tossed to the side like a sack of potatoes. He was asking me to go deliver a message to this man to let him know how much he had hurt him. Imagine this scene: Jill walks over to the unsuspecting man attempting to enjoy his glass of wine while his favorite band is playing. "Excuse me, sir. Do you remember going home one night with a guy named Joe? Well, Joe is on the Other Side now and would like you to know how much you hurt him. He says to tell you that it would be really good if you would start thinking of others' feelings and not just your own selfish needs." Needless to say, I did not deliver Joe's message! Instead, I continued arguing with him throughout the evening because he thought he could talk me into delivering his message to Matt. How many people have argued with a Spirit in a bar? This is not something you normally hear about! Yet these are situations that we mediums deal with all the time.

While we are on the subject of drinking and barriers coming down, let me share some of my experiences when I took an Uber. Several times, the Spirit Communicators have followed me out of a bar and into the car. This actually happened with the agitated Spirit of Joe. He followed me out of that wine bar and into the Uber. Yup, Joe was right there with me and my husband in the car. I continued my conversation with him out loud while my husband talked to the Uber driver. The poor guy kept turning around, craning his neck to see where in the back seat that third person might be hiding out! He had seen only two people get into his car! I continued trying to reason with Joe throughout the several miles to our destination. As my husband and I exited the back of the Uber, the driver turned around and said, "Did everyone get out of the car?" I'm sure he was ready to drop me off at the nearest mental institution.

Many times, I have just ended up reading the Uber drivers. Of course, I ask for their permission first. I have told them about job changes they have coming up, or a child that has yet to be conceived. I have brought family members through with beautiful messages. Again, we mediums do our best to keep our boundaries up, but when I have had wine or beer, those boundaries drop quickly and the floodgates open. Because of this, I rarely drink anymore, as I find it exhausting to my human energy field. As mediums, our physical bodies serve as vessels through which Spirit communicates. It is therefore imperative that we keep these vessels as clean and pure as possible. However, as human beings, we sometimes just want to *be* normal and enjoy a cocktail or two!

Another dynamic of being a medium is how we feel energy. Which is to say, we *feel* it all the time. Always. Without fail. We can walk into a room and immediately sense the energy. Does it *feel* calm? Does it *feel* angry or sad? We have spent our whole lives paying attention to how something or someone feels to us. We honestly don't know any other way to be. Again, until a medium studies with a mentor and learns how to protect their auric field, it can be quite draining to always feel everything around them. Until they learn how to handle this, most of the time they are sensing the feelings of people around them, not understanding that the emotion does not even belong to them. One of my psychic colleagues went through therapy to learn which emotions were hers and which ones belonged to everyone else she came into contact with. If you can recognize this to be your own truth and reality, I encourage you to find a psychic to study with. Most people who pursue intuitive development programs are doing so to help them live with their sensitivities. With the right teacher and mentor, you can learn to take good care of your own auric field.

We also pay attention to signs and synchronicities. We know that our loved ones and guardian angels like to guide us by showing us signs. We have learned to pay attention to these signs. We follow number patterns such as 1111 or 444. We understand that numbers hold a certain energetic vibration and the Spirit World can use numbers to communicate with us. This is where the term "Pennies from Heaven" comes from. Some of our loved ones leave nickels and dimes too. I keep asking my mom to leave some $100 bills, but so far, no luck!

I know for myself, that when things happen multiple times or there is a synchronicity to something, I pay attention. This was not always the case. One of my Spirit Guides told me that it took years for me to pay attention! I was told that I was so hardheaded that I needed to be hit over the head with an etheric two-by-four before I would pay attention to the signs they were trying to give me! Trust me, I learned the hard way. I listen and pay attention now. Life is much easier this way.

I invite you to pay attention to the signs and synchronicities in your life. The term synchronicity was coined by famed psychiatrist Carl Jung to describe simultaneous or closely occurring complementary events (often considered coincidences) which apparently have no clear cause but are deeply meaningful. Our loved ones and Spirit Guides definitely send us signs. It's true what they say about there being no accidents. Synchronicities may also show up to help us make decisions, or connect us with someone, or to simply inspire us. Signs from our loved ones may also come through music or songs.

Our Angels and Guides have volunteered to help and guide us. However, they will never stand in the way of our free will. If we ask for their help, they are always there. I encourage each of you to start paying attention to signs and synchronicities in your life. Ask your Guides to guide your way. As long as your requests coincide with your original life path and contracts, they are happy to help. As souls, we have chosen to experience growth and learning opportunities with each lifetime. Again, this is not for punishment. It is our own freewill choice in order to grow in consciousness and our soul's evolution. For example, if you have purposely chosen a lifetime of knowing what it is like to experience financial challenge, you are probably not going to talk your angels into helping you win the lottery! For me personally, I chose not to have the experience of being a biological mother in this lifetime. During the years of five miscarriages and the heartache and sorrow that comes with each one, I was not aware that I had made this decision before I incarnated this time around. It was through getting my certification in past-life regression in Sedona, Arizona, that I came to realize I had not been the best parent in most of my lifetimes. So, my soul chose to experience a lifetime of not being a biological parent. Over the years, I have found that even when faced with the greatest of challenges, we are always given a silver lining. For me, my silver lining came in an unexpected way. I helped raise my stepson Austin, who decided to start calling me Mom when he was in the seventh grade. Austin and I have shared many past lives together. When Austin was five, and my ex-husband introduced us for the first time, Austin asked him, "When do we get to move in with Jill"? Our souls recognized each other immediately! I have come to realize that you can be an amazing parent even if your parenthood is not biological. Austin has been one of my greatest gifts and helping to raise him one of my proudest accomplishments.

One misconception most people have about psychics is that we know everything – or at least more than is considered "natural." If I had a dollar for every time someone asked me why I had not yet won the lottery if I'm such a great psychic, I would be rich. Our gifts do not work this way. They are not for our personal gain. We chose areas of growth opportunities to learn from in this lifetime too. Just because we are psychic does not mean we are not human. As an example, I have not made the wisest choices in the past where relationships were concerned. I have had my share of "learning opportunities" with my love life! Don't you just love that euphemism? Learning opportunities sounds so much better than screw-ups or failed relationships! Seriously, though, most of these relationships had to do with past lives and balancing karma. Or helping me to grow as a soul. Thankfully, those hard lessons are behind me now as I am married to my twin flame Daniel. I dedicate an entire chapter to Daniel later in the book.

Even though we have our own soul growth opportunities to experience and many times our Guides will not interfere, there are times when they do. I vividly remember two occasions when my Spirit Guides did specifically tell me about my cheating partners. The first was a relationship I had right after college. The man was bilingual, from South America. We married and moved to Florida. I began to suspect he was cheating on me, but I could not prove it and he continued to deny it. As a backstory, he owned an import /export company and worked from a home office, so our phone bill was usually about 20 to 30 pages long, with numerous international numbers. One morning at about 5:00 a.m., I was in a twilight kind of sleep when I heard my Guide talking to me. I was told, *You are correct -- he is cheating. Get up and find the latest phone bill. Turn to page 15 and look at the phone numbers on that page. I will tell you which number to call. His Spanish girlfriend will answer the phone.* I got out of bed and found the phone bill and did as I was instructed. About halfway down the page, I was told to stop and dial the number. A woman answered. I knew enough Spanish to ask her if she was having a relationship with my then-husband. She said yes. When I told her that he was married to me, she started crying. Needless to say, I left that marriage.

Another instance of my Spirit Guides warning me about something happened when I was married to Austin's father. One night I was in bed reading, and my then-husband was downstairs watching TV. As clear as a bell, my guides said to me, *Ann has just started working with your husband and she is trying to start an affair with him. It is important that you warn him and ask him not to fall victim to her flirtations.* I marched downstairs and with hand on hip asked, "Who is Ann?" My ex looks up from the TV and reports, "I don't know an Ann." Me: "Yes, you do. She just started working with you." My ex lights up and says, "Oh, you mean Anna." Me: "Ann, Anna, whatever her name is, she is going to try to have an affair with you. We are not doing well in our marriage, but please don't go down that road." My ex reassures me, "She's not my type. You have nothing to worry about." Ladies let me digress for a moment here before I continue. It does not take a psychic to know that most of the time when we are told this, it is not true. Pay attention to your gut feelings. My Guides had this conversation with me in December. Three months later, in March, I found a mushy love card from Anna in my now ex-husband's car.

I decided to call sweet Anna and tell her how thoughtful and well received her card to my husband had been, and how much her sentiments meant to us. She admitted everything and actually said, "We were both pretty freaked out that you knew this would happen before it even happened." I said, "And yet you thought it was a great idea anyway to have an affair with the husband of a psychic medium? Did you think I wouldn't know?" Sweet Anna did not seem in the slightest way remorseful. I could hear those wheels of karma spinning!

Given that my Spirit Guides are always so vocal about situations they want me to be aware of, are you wondering why they didn't just save me the heartache from the beginning by tipping me off before I married these men?

Such "help" would tamper with karma and past-life issues that need balancing. My soul and theirs chose to come together in this lifetime for mutual learning and growth. Ideally, we would not have to suffer -- regardless of past-life tendencies -- as the choice for faithfulness is always possible.

Over my years of doing this work, there have been many amazing readings that changed lives. One that comes to mind happened just after I first moved to Asheville, NC. One day, I was in a temporary vacation rental, enjoying its backyard. I heard a woman crying in the yard next door. I walked over and asked if she was okay. She explained that she and her husband had lost their granddaughter the day before in a motorcycle accident. She'd been about to graduate from high school around the time of her accident. I explained to her that I am a medium and would be happy to gift her with a session. I told her we should wait a month or so to give her granddaughter time to get settled in and acclimated to the other side before I attempted to connect with her. I have had loved ones come through the day after they passed. However, for professional sittings, I generally recommend waiting three months. This gives our loved ones time to learn how to work with the energy of connecting to a medium; it also gives the bereaved time to process some of their grief. The grandmother told me she would love nothing more than for me to connect with her granddaughter; however, her husband was a skeptic. As I was leaving that vacation rental a few weeks later, I gave the grandmother my card. I told her to call me if she ever changed her mind, that the offer was still good, and that there would be no charge. About three months later, I received a call from her. She told me her husband had agreed to the reading. She explained that he still did not believe in mediums but was willing to sit through it for her. A week later, I entered a house filled with family and friends. There must have been 15 people there! OK, Jill, I told myself. No pressure here! You have just stepped into a potential lion's den with at least one diehard skeptic in the mix, and there are 15 people waiting anxiously to see if you can really deliver.

Please indulge me as I go on a quick tangent here before I continue with the story. For those who write articles saying that all the medium ever says is that she loved you dearly and is guiding you from above, let me please give you the 411 on the truth. Trust me -- when people are sitting right in front of you, waiting to hear from their loved one, they are expecting names, approximate age when the person passed, and cause of death – was it an accident or illness? Also desired and expected are facts about their personality and habits, and memories that the medium would have no way of knowing. If the reader can't provide these details, they do not stay in business very long.

Okay, thank you for entertaining my rant. Now we can rejoin the grandparents, friends, and family of the young girl who died in a motorcycle accident. I don't remember all the details from the reading. Most of the time, the information is wiped clean from my psyche right after the reading is over. This time, I do recall that the connection was amazing. The granddaughter provided tons of evidence, and there were many tears shed during the session. Toward the end, the skeptical grandfather said to me, "Ask her who has her motorcycle helmet?" I did ask the girl and her response was, "Tell my grandpa that I know he has my helmet and that this makes me unbelievably happy." Her grandfather started sobbing. After the reading, he walked over to me and asked if he could hug me. He told me that I had just changed his life. He was now a believer in the afterlife. He explained how comforting it was going to be for him knowing his granddaughter was in heaven and doing well.

Another session I recall was from when I was a speaker on an Intuition Cruise in April 2017. I was giving private readings and a woman came to me for a session. I brought her friend Rick through, who told me he had recently passed from a heart attack. She told me that I was mistaken because her friend Rick was alive and well. I went ahead and delivered the messages to her from Rick. She emailed me after she got home from the cruise and found out that sure enough, her friend Rick had passed away from a heart attack the week before our cruise.

Sometimes the evidence we are given as mediums is comical. A session where I brought through a woman's husband comes to mind. He kept saying to me, *Talk to my wife about the monkeys*. I figured I was hearing him wrong, so I didn't deliver the message at first. He was persistent. He finally exclaimed, "TELL her I'm talking about the monkeys!" I finally reluctantly relayed the message. She started crying and laughing at the same time. He collected toy monkeys, and she had one of his favorite monkey statues buried with him in his coffin. Tell a skeptic to put *that* specific evidence in his pipe and smoke it!

I still laugh as I recall a session that I gave to a husband. His wife came through with a great deal of validating evidence, and her message to him was that she wanted him to move on and to find companionship again. She did not want him to be alone or lonely. Not skipping a beat, the widower turned to me and said (with all seriousness), "Okay, will you go out with me? You are very pretty." Are you kidding me? I turned to him and said, "Sir, I am speaking to your wife right now. Please don't make this anymore awkward for me than it already is. And no, I will not be going out with you."

As I mentioned earlier, this work is a calling. Most of us do not wake up one day and decide we are going to be a psychic medium. We have no choice in the matter. We *are* mediums. Having free will, we can of course deny who we are and choose to withhold our services. At times, it is not an easy road. I recall one of my favorite mediumship teachers, Mavis Pittilla, posing a certain question to the group. The group consisted of about 50 mediums from all over the country who were there for an advanced mediumship training program. Her question burns deep in my soul to this day. She'd asked, "How many of you have attempted to leave the world of mediumship?" About three-quarters of the students raised their hands. She chuckled and said, "How has that worked out for you?" It was unanimous: trying to walk away does not work out well at all. We will always be mediums. There are days where it feels like the grief and sadness of our clients will bury us alive. There are days when the responsibility of it weighs on my body like the armor of a soldier going into battle. Yet, it is the most beautiful honor I can imagine. Having the gift of being able to connect one who is grieving with their loved one in the Spirit World is the most precious privilege I can think of. To be the voice for the Other World is a wonderful life purpose. I never take my gift for granted. I always remain humble. Even though I am changing lives through this gift, I always remind myself that I am simply the conduit. I am the channel.

I AM the medium.

Chapter 3

Jumping Off the Cliff

Southern California. I was living the dream. Or so I thought at the time. I was a woman who had truly made it in her field. I was a female CPA and business manager in Hollywood. Sunshine, money, and movie stars, oh my! Did I mention the money? I had the million-dollar house, the Mercedes, the Rolex, and lots of money flowing in. I was a personal signer on bank accounts totaling in the hundreds of thousands of dollars. I was invited to movie premieres and Hollywood parties. My bank invited me to sit in their private box at Staples Center in Hollywood because my clients and I had so much money in their bank.

So, if my life was so grand, what happened to change all that?

Before I get to that part of the story, let me take you down memory lane and relive some of the high points. First, for those of you who do not know what a business manager is, let me explain. A business manager in Hollywood is someone who manages the money of wealthy, successful actors, directors, voice-over actors, stuntmen and women, writers, and producers. These clients all have one thing in common. They are successful and either do not know how to manage all the money or choose not to worry about it. That's where a business manager comes in. For a small percentage of their income paid to the manager, their monthly bills are paid, tax and financial planning is put in place, houses and cars are negotiated, and best-case-scenario wealth is created in a way that ensures they never need to work again, if they choose not to.

This was an exciting and glamorous time in my life. I recall being invited to accompany one of my clients to her movie premiere in Las Vegas. We were picked up by limo and driven to the airport. When we landed in Las Vegas, another limo was waiting to whisk us off to the hotel. My childlike excitement must have been evident when I saw the penthouse suite we'd be staying in. Room service flowed like a river run wild with anything we desired. I was introduced to many other of the movie's celebrities. I would not be truthful if I said this entire incident was not exhilarating to experience.

Another fond memory is of a huge party thrown by one of the production companies. This party was for the children of the people connected to the productions. I was given enough tickets to bring my stepson Austin who was eight at the time, and my sister's two children, Payton and Reagan, nine and seven years old. The four of us were picked up by limo and driven to the party. The terms "out of this world" and "over the top" – especially for the kids! – seem about right. Amidst all the rides, food, and entertainment, a young pop star, who is now very well known, held a concert outside for the kids.

I even ended up living in the same gated community one of my wealthy clients was living in! The way this unfolded was crazy, yet shows how powerful a manifestor I am when I don't allow my fears to block me. I was renting, and decided I was ready to purchase my first home. Before I started looking, I went to a professional psychic whom I would see from time to time. And yes, we psychics do go to other psychics. It's difficult to see the forest for the trees at times in our personal lives. She told me all about the house I would purchase. As her reading progressed, she saw a gated community, and I started laughing. Do you know how much it costs to live in a gated community in California? I told her to keep going, but I thought she was mistaken. She went on to explain that the way it came to pass would be extraordinary. She told me that the house I would buy had fallen out of escrow from an attorney who had bought it. She also asserted that as I was walking through the community, I would see trees still in their boxes waiting to be planted. I paid for the session and went on my way, thinking wow! She is so far off on this!

A few months later, one of my clients asked me to go with her for a final walkthrough of her brand-new home. As we drove through the gates of this community, I admired its beauty. We then stopped in at the sales office to go over some paperwork. The saleswoman looked at me and said, "Why don't you purchase here too?" I started laughing and said, "I'm doing well for myself, but not *that* well! Not yet, anyway." Seemingly on script, the woman said, "We just had an attorney who backed out of his house right before it went to escrow." My psychic antennae shot up. I asked, "Did I hear you correctly? You say you have a house that just fell out of escrow from an attorney?" She said, yes, and that it was in the least expensive part of the community. This section featured the more affordable homes; another area included those in the middle range, and the third section was given over to exclusive estates. My client was overjoyed at the idea of us living in the same community. So, I thought okay, how will it hurt to just walk over there and take a look? As the three of us were heading for the house, I began to notice the trees in boxes that had not yet been planted. Now my psychic apparatus was on high alert. This was unfolding exactly as the psychic had predicted. How could this be? More to the point, how was I supposed to afford this grandeur? All the while, a little voice in my head was saying, *just trust and surrender.* The saleswoman went on to say that since this one was already sold and they were almost finished with the development, they were offering a ridiculously low-down payment. As I stood on the balcony of the master bedroom looking out over the mountains, I knew I was home. I called my mom and said, "I'm buying a house in Angela's community!" Predictably, Mom asked, "How are you going to pull this off?" I said, "The Universe wants me here, so it will deliver the resources necessary." I then informed her that she would be moving in with me so we could pool our funds and afford the mortgage! My mom -- who knew me so very well -- then said, "J, you are crazy, but let's do this." And so it was that my beautiful mom and I moved into this brand-new home in that gated community. You can be sure that we went on to have some inspiring times together!

It is my hope that by sharing this story of an amazing manifestation, you will remember how powerful a creator you are as well. This does not suggest that we go out and act impulsively or irresponsibly, taking on more than we can handle. What it does mean is that when the Universe hands us lemons, we make the best damned lemonade on the planet, baby! When something falls into place effortlessly, that is a huge sign that it is meant to be. It's when we try to force that proverbial square peg again and again into a round hole that we get into trouble. Some of us even go so far as to slice off the edges of the square peg to make it fit into the round hole! Forcing matters never works. When something doesn't fall smoothly into place, learn to walk away.

Let me give you some words of wisdom about the messages you may receive from a psychic reading. Sometimes it takes months or even years for certain messages to make sense or materialize. This may happen for several reasons. First, time and space are of a 3-D reality. In the Spirit World, time doesn't work the same way that it does on the physical plane. Therefore, when a loved one or even a Spirit Guide is providing details and shedding light on a situation, the timing may be way off. Second, we each have free will. A psychic can tune in to the aura of someone in any given moment and can see past-life karma and soul contracts, or the lack thereof, and from this infer the probability of something manifesting between two people. However, free will is always present. Just because one member of a soul mate duo "remembers" the soul contract, doesn't necessarily mean that the other does too. Or maybe the other does remember and has the knowing, yet is not ready to step up to the plate and bring their full monty to the table. (As I'm writing this, I realize that full monty is not a term I have ever used, nor would I use it. I had to look it up to see if I am even using it in the proper context. It turns out, this is a British slang phrase and guess what? My main Spirit Guide Saisha just happens to be British! Thank you, Saisha, for spicing up my words!) The third reason timing may be off is that the client or sitter doesn't take any of the guidance offered and move forward with it. I can't tell you the number of times I have given a reading where the person is asking about meeting a lover or mate. As an example, I would tune in and be shown that they meet at an outdoor event with the sun shining brightly. I encourage my client to attend any and all such events they can think of or are invited to. Fast-forward six months and my client calls for another reading, asking the same question about meeting their love. They tell me my prediction has not come to pass. I then ask how many outdoor events they have attended. Silence. How many? I ask. None, they say. Okay, so I am a psychic, not a miracle worker. I can't conjure up the ideal man or woman and teleport them to the backyard of my client's home. I'm good but I'm not that good! Folks, when you get guidance from a psychic who has been accurate about other matters, pay attention to the details!

There is not a psychic on the planet who can guarantee that so-and-so is your one and only soul mate, destined to marry you. If you go to a psychic who guarantees you something like this, run -- don't walk -- away. And if you are asked to pay extra money for them to put a love-spell on someone, run away even faster.

One way you can tune in to see if the guidance you are receiving is accurate is to see if you "feel" the accuracy of the message. Some people get goose bumps. Some get chills. Some may even feel the energy shift in the room. However, please don't get caught up in thinking something does not make sense just because in that moment it doesn't *seem to* make sense. Things take time to unfold. Just be sure to never give your power away to anyone, and certainly not to a psychic. You are a free agent, your own individual person. I always tell my clients, please make sure everything resonates as truth for you. Tune in yourself and then listen. Some of the most powerful sessions I have ever given were when the information coming through the Spirit World simply validated everything my clients had been thinking themselves!

A major part of the joy I get from teaching psychic and intuitive development is watching my students learning to trust themselves and the messages they are receiving from their Higher Self or their Spirit Guides. In my humble opinion, everyone should take an excellent course in intuitive development! Most students who take my courses do not plan to hang up a shingle offering their services. Most are simply wanting to make better life decisions by learning discernment, and how to connect with their Angels and Guides. The transformation I witness in my students is truly miraculous. Typically, they begin Level 1 feeling fear, not trusting their own messages or guidance; by the end of the program, most students are confidently bringing forth messages from their personal Spirit Team! Those lucky enough to come in person to our Mississippi Intuitive Academy receive the benefit of learning from two seasoned psychics! Duann Kier and I have created a Psychic Development Program together that is truly out of this world, if I do say so myself! Participating in a good intuitive/psychic development program can change your life in ways you can't imagine. I encourage you to find one in your city or state or, better yet, plan on traveling to Mississippi to participate in ours!

One dynamic in our lives that seems to strengthen when we tap into our personal intuition is that of trust and surrender. I am going to give you one of the great keys to a successful life: Learn to trust and surrender. But before you can trust, you must learn to distinguish trustworthy, intuitive guidance from the clamoring of your ego. Again, this is something a great intuitive development course can teach you. Once you learn to trust, the next step is to surrender. Ah, that pesky little word, *surrender*. According to Paramahansa Yogananda, spiritual surrender means self-offering of one's will to God. This is far from being passive. It is actually the opposite of passive. The moment we step into the trust of surrender is the moment of self-empowering illumination. When we learn to pay attention to the signs and synchronicities of the Universe, true magic unfolds. And in those powerful, breathtaking moments when we stand witness to this magic, we realize that we are powerful spiritual beings capable of creating masterpieces. In my opinion, a must-read for everyone is *Autobiography of a Yogi*, by Paramahansa Yogananda. Reading this book helps you grasp the little-known fact that we are capable of extraordinary feats and wonders that defy the logic of all that we have been told.

Okay, now back to the story of my previous life of Riley. I could go on and on with examples of the perks of rubbing elbows with celebrities. But I'm sure you get the picture. You may wonder, if life was such a dream, why did I merrily stop rowing my boat and leave it all behind? Because Spirit had other plans for me. My own soul had made a soul contract before I incarnated to comfort, educate, and inspire through spiritual and mediumship sessions, teaching, and writing. I just had not "remembered" this yet.

When we are not on our true paths, we can have our memories jogged in many ways. For some, it's the loss of a job. For others, it's a spouse leaving the marriage, or even a spouse transitioning to the Other Side. Others have lost children. For me, it was through illness. I almost died. I ended up in the hospital twice. Not once. Twice. Why did it take two stays, you may ask? Because I was one of those hardheaded types. Remember the etheric two-by-four to get my attention!

My health started to decline from the stress I was under. Many of my Hollywood clients were not kind all the time. In fact, they could be quite demanding. I remember one who was a director on a well-known television show. His ex-wife knew how to manipulate him and was constantly charging up the credit cards and overdrawing her bank account. The alimony he gave her was staggering, yet it wasn't enough for her. He was constantly instructing us to send more money to her. I tried to counsel him about boundaries and how her overspending and overdrafts were not his problem. My counseling seemed to bounce off deaf ears. However, when it was time to pay his monthly income taxes from his substantial paycheck, he found it therapeutic to call and yell at me. He unleashed all his fury from his lack of boundaries with his ex-wife, and I was the lucky punching bag. He ranted and raved about how much he had to pay in income taxes. At one point I sarcastically said, "I have a solution for you. You trade your paycheck for my paycheck, and I will gladly pay the taxes on your paycheck." Strange thing is, he never took me up on my offer. Point made. Yet the yelling continued.

There were husbands and wives with gambling problems and secrets that I was instructed to keep secret from their spouses. I watched one very talented artist's finances dwindle down to nothing due to his gambling addiction.

In my situation, it seemed to be the more well-known actors who were the nicest. These clients made my job much easier and I truly appreciated their kindness. You could easily determine who was going to continue on in the public eye doing what they love. On the other hand, you didn't need a crystal ball to tell which ones were going to self-combust. And quite a few did. They could not handle the instant fame or the lightning-bolt arrival of wealth.

I'm sure there are many business managers who do not feel the pressure I did. When we are on the path of what we came here to do, we don't feel the debilitating stress in our work that others may. Since I was giving my heart and soul to something that I had not made a soul contract to do, my stress began to affect my physical health. I started feeling extreme fatigue. My joints were very painful. At times, it felt as if I were trying to walk through quicksand. I started gaining weight and losing my hair. My hands and feet were always cold. It took years before the doctors figured it out. I was diagnosed with lupus, the same disease that took my gran's life when she was only 52 years old. Looking back now, I realize the lupus didn't take my grandmother's life. It was the effects of the harmful pharmaceuticals that killed her.

As you can probably imagine, I was in complete shock. But I kept pushing forward and persevering. I wasn't going to allow my health to slow me down. Before long, the pain became unbearable. I was then diagnosed with degenerative disc disease and told I needed major back and neck surgery or else I would be paralyzed. I will never forget the neurosurgeon who came into the examination room bowing her head and telling me how sorry she was. She delivered the verdict that I would eventually be paralyzed. She then explained a dangerous surgical option that also held the risk of paralysis. I remember going home and sobbing for hours. At one point, I was taking eight pain pills a day. My health was spiraling out of control.

One of my darkest hours came when I almost died. I was in the hospital because I was having difficulty breathing. It was clear that if I kept on with the pills and path I was on, I would be making my transition to the Spirit World. Shortly after this last hospital close call, I heard about a Reiki Master healer named Joan. I was out of options, so in desperation, I scheduled a session with her. She explained that because I was on so much medication, I would need three sessions to start with. At that point in my declining health, I probably would have jumped off the Empire State Building if someone had promised me better health (and a safety net) at the bottom. I happily made the three appointments. What happened in that first session changed my life in countless ways. I started "remembering" my life mission and what I came here to do. It didn't all come flooding in at once, but a key was turned in that session and I knew I would never go backwards. By session two, I was ready to get off all of my medication. Joan instructed me that I would need to do this slowly and in a safe manner per doctor's instructions.

I started taking Reiki classes and eventually attained my Reiki Master Certification. I then got certified in past-life regression and tarot. I was stepping into the truth of who I was. I stopped eating animals and my health grew stronger. I started losing weight without even trying. My energy was coming back. I knew what was next on my path. I could no longer be a CPA/business manager. I came here to be of service to the Spirit World and to the many people seeking spiritual guidance and connections with their loved ones. My now ex-husband wasn't quite as overjoyed when I relayed this exciting news to him. He said, "I married a CPA, not a psychic." I corrected him: "No, you married a psychic who just happened to be a CPA when you married her." He'd been a skeptic throughout our marriage, yet to his credit, years after our divorce, he admitted that my gifts had made a believer out of him.

I fondly recall rehearsing the phone call that I would make to my dad, explaining the new direction of my life. "Dad," I began warmly. "I truly appreciate the college degree that you paid for me to attain, but I have decided to sell my CPA firm and become a professional psychic." Dead silence. Nothing for at least 120 long seconds. "Dad, are you there?" My amazing dad then says to me, "I only want for you to be happy, and if this is what is going to make you happy, then I support you 100%." After I hung up the phone, I cried for many reasons. I shed tears because I finally felt free. I also realized how very blessed I am to have chosen the parents that I did. Once I had "come out of the psychic closet," one of my teachers told me that I received my mediumship gifts from Mom and my psychic gifts from Dad. When I shared this insight with my dad, it really resonated with him! He explained how throughout his life and especially in business situations, he would know and see things that others couldn't see, and how frustrating it was for him that they couldn't see what he could see. He laughed when he added, "I didn't know how I knew; I just knew! So, I guess the cat's out of the bag now!"

As I journeyed into professional psychic mediumship, my dad continued to be one of my biggest fans. He faithfully listened to every one of my shows during the years I hosted my own radio program, *Connect Soul to Soul*. He would call me after each show and give me feedback, including constructive critiques when needed. Dad's support and assistance during these years means more to me than he can possibly imagine. It was my father who paid for me to travel to Arthur Findlay College in England and study with some of the most gifted mediums of our time. He paid for me to study at Lily Dale, Omega, and The Journey Within, in New Jersey. Those intense classes took my mediumship gifts to the next level. I would not be the medium I am today without the help from my dad.

My relationship with Dad over the years had had its ups and downs for sure. However, the bond we now share can never be broken. I owe Dad my understanding of ethics, and my commitment to honesty. Growing up, if my sister and I did something we were not supposed to do and then admitted to it, we would still get punished, but not for as long. Part of our "sentence" was pardoned for being honest! My dad also instilled in us the value of never giving up. I remember him stressing that you fail only if you quit trying. These words of wisdom have served me so well in my life. Dad taught me to believe in myself. And he taught (and showed) me the necessity for humor! Laughter is vitally important, and after so many conversations with the Spirit

World, I have learned that our loved ones want us to laugh and have fun!

I have been guided to include a poem I wrote for my dad a couple of years ago on Father's Day. Please know that I am not a poet; however, the feelings I poured out still fill my heart with joy whenever I read this.

From the beginning of time, I looked up to you.
Who knew in that moment, all we would go through?
Like waves from an ocean and sands of time,
When I reflect on you, Dad, the result is sublime.
Even though there were mistakes and times of pain,
The strength of our bond was the real gain.
I need you to know what a gift you have been,
You continually taught me that truth lies within.
Thank you for always believing in me,
Giving me wings, so I could fly free.
Today, on Father's Day, I want you to know,
We have come full circle from so long ago.
Just as the moon glows and the sun shines its rays.
I honor you, Dad, and will love you always.

In closing this chapter, I would like to invite each of you to delve deep and discover your life path and what you have come here to do. Honor the truth of who you are. Change can be quite frightening. Always remember, in the words of Pierre Teilhard de Chardin, that you are strong, "a spiritual being, having a human experience." Borrow a little courage from others who have changed course later in life, or who went with the Universe's way to change it for them. Walt Disney was fired from his job as a newspaper cartoonist because it was said he "lacked imagination and had no good ideas." Julia Child worked for the CIA and didn't write her first cookbook until she was 50. Vera Wang was a figure skater and did not even enter the field of fashion until she was over 40. Grandma Moses was in her late 70s when she gifted the world with her first painting. One of her creations later sold for $1.2 million dollars. It is never too late to follow your dream or to "remember" your soul purpose.

Have the courage to trust your intuition and change the course of your voyage, if necessary. Know that your angel wings will grow to support your flight as long as the journey is in alignment with your soul contracts. Go within, my friends, and find the true north of your intuitive compass.

Chapter 4

Best American Psychics

A few years after I had come out of the closet as a professional psychic, I found out about a directory for psychics and mediums called *Best American Psychics*. I had heard of other directories, but this one was different. This directory double-blind tests all their psychics and mediums and performs background and website checks. All must meet rigorous ethical standards and demonstrate their giftedness before being welcomed into this exclusive club. A friend told me I should apply for membership.

As I processed this recommendation, my stomach dropped. After all, this was about to get real! What would I do if I did not pass the two blind readings? As most people agree, any type of "test" is frightening. But a test that basically reveals whether you are accurate enough to be among the top in your profession? My first thought was, *thank you, but no thank you!* I prayed and meditated on this opportunity and was told to just trust and surrender to Spirit. I completed the application quickly so I would not chicken out! Soon after, I received my two test dates along with the time each of the sitters would call me for their reading. A sitter is the person receiving the reading. We were not even given a first name. I completed both readings and waited what seemed like a lifetime for the email to arrive letting me know whether I passed or not. I can't begin to describe the unbelievable joy when I found out I'd been accepted! I was now a member of the *Best American Psychics*! To highlight what an honor this was, some of the members of the Lifetime Achievement Awards are Hans Christian King, Michelle Whitedove, John Holland, and James Van Praagh. I later learned that only a small percentage of applicants are accepted into this exclusive organization. I'm thankful I wasn't aware of this fact before I tested.

You'll recall that Shay Parker is the founder of *Best American Psychics*. Initially a skeptic, Shay admits that she has always been a very left-brained individual, with most of her work having been in finance. The "paranormal" or "metaphysical" world was more or less foreign to her; she neither believed nor disbelieved. In Shay's mind, there was not much room for "spirits, ghosts, or spooks" after crunching numbers all day long and having to meet end-of-month deadlines.

However, it was obviously part of Shay's soul contract to bring awareness and professionalism to the paranormal. The Universe has a way of providing opportunities and openings to help us navigate our life path. The Universe provided this very opening for Shay when she least expected it.

When Shay moved into a 100+-year-old cabin in the mountains of Asheville, NC, unexplainable things began to occur that were noticed not only by her, but others as well. At first her logical mind dismissed all the odd events as imagination, coincidence, electrical issues, etc. But when the phenomena began to escalate; all logic fell short. Shay was forced to accept that she was living in a haunted cabin, and there was no way around it. She could actually hear the spirits talking, and then they even began to physically touch her -- not in a bad or threatening way, but definitely perceptible touch -- an encouraging hand on a shoulder or an affectionate pat on the head could come at any time.

At that point, Shay knew she needed to do something about it, but had no idea where to turn or whom to call. And no, for those of you who are perhaps media-savvy, she did not call Ghostbusters! She turned to a medium who was eventually able to help solve the issues for her. The encounter and experience with the medium sparked something new in Shay -- a curiosity to see beyond the black-and-white numbers on her computer screen. She wanted to know what these spirits wanted, and why (and how) it was that they were able to communicate with her to the point of sound and touch. This was an almost inconceivable reality, way beyond her comfort level.

Her quest took her to create a place that could bring much-needed attention to some of the amazing people she was coming in contact with. These folks were very gifted, real people who, yes, could see and talk to the dead, or to spirit guides. Thus, *Best American Psychics* was born.

I find it so fascinating and enchanting the way doors miraculously open for us to show the way to our life path, majestically appearing right in front of us. The key is to pay attention. I shudder to think what would have happened if Shay had not paid attention to the intuitive whispers given by her own spirit guides. There is a running joke among the *Best American Psychics* -- Bappers," as we are affectionately referred to. Shay claims she is not psychic, but the psychics on her team know better! Yet, it was not in Shay's soul contract to offer her services as a professional psychic, but rather to provide a forum where the best psychics and mediums in the United States could join forces, offering a safe resource for those seeking spiritual guidance.

Best American Psychics gives annual awards to acknowledge service and excellence above and beyond. In 2014, I was awarded the Social Activism Award for my work with animals. This was especially poignant for me because the animal kingdom has my heart and soul. Part of my soul contract is to be the voice for the animals who have no voice. My quest and vision are that one day all animals will be seen and understood as the sentient beings they are.

In the spring of 2014, I received a call from Shay Parker asking me if I would communicate with a horse she had just rescued. Immediately my stomach dropped to my feet. No pressure at all, Jill! The founder of *Best American Psychics* is asking you to read her horse. All manner of fears flooded in: What if I suck? What if I can't connect in a way that benefits Shay and her horse? These are normal fears that we psychics go through from time to time. As some colleagues have said, you are only as good as your last reading. I remember the day well when I asked my mom to accompany me to meet Shay and her sister Angel at the barn. I can't say I was shaking in my boots because I wasn't wearing boots, but I can reveal that my nerves were on overdrive. As I have learned to do, I took a deep breath and asked my human self and ego self to step aside in order for Spirit to work through me. I will share the testimonial from Shay to best describe what happened.

"This is Shay Parker and I want to share my recent experience with Psychic Medium and Animal Communicator Jill M. Jackson. About a week ago, I had the honor of rescuing a young horse (Shakespeare) that was living in very bad conditions. I did not have a clear picture of what his background was, and I really had no idea of his state of mind.

"After moving him to his new barn, I asked Jill if she would do an animal communication session with him so that I could get a better idea of his story. Jill's session with him was amazing. It was very informative, and she communicated a lot of detailed information.

"Early in the session, Jill asked Shakespeare if he was happy at his new home. He immediately "showed" her a bolt of lightning, and how it really frightened him. She said that it was very recent, and he was quite afraid of it. She then asked me if he showed any signs of fear around the rain or storms. I explained that I was not sure, because I had known him for only 48 hours.

"I remember thinking that he had not yet experienced a storm at the new barn, to my knowledge. However, Jill was very clear and kept describing "a large bolt of lightning.

"The session continued, and we moved on to other things. After Jill left, the owner of the stables came up and started talking to me. Her attention was focused on the round pen which was out in the pasture. I had noticed earlier that the round pen had a wooden board that had fallen off the top rung. The owner asked me if I knew what happened. I looked at her very puzzled and explained that I did not go anywhere near the round pen.

"Then, as if a light bulb went off, she quickly exclaimed, 'Oh my goodness, that is what it struck!' Again, I was confused, and I asked her what she was talking about. She then explained that they had had a terrible storm the night before and her husband was standing on her porch looking over the farm. He said a huge bolt of lightning struck down in the pasture and a loud snap occurred. She concluded that the lightning bolt struck the round pen and knocked the top rail off. She also went over and checked the electric fence, and it had been blown. Upon further inspection of the round pen, you could see the burn marks from where the lightning struck it.

"I could not believe what I was hearing because, not 20 minutes earlier, Jill had explained that Shakespeare was showing her a huge bolt of lightning and was afraid of it.

"How is that for instant validation of evidential information? If anyone out there wishes to connect with their pet, either here or passed over, or needs a psychic reading on a human level, I cannot say enough about Jill M. Jackson. I witnessed firsthand her abilities, and her incredible accuracy." Shay Parker, May 23, 2014.

Some of my favorite readings over the years have been with animals. They have great personalities and have lots to say when given the chance! I have communicated with dogs, cats, horses, chickens, goats, birds, donkeys, cows, and pigs. Communicating with these amazing sentient beings is one of the main factors in my converting to plant-based eating. How could I possibly chat with a pig about his likes and dislikes and then devour a BLT later in the day that had been a pig who didn't get the chance to communicate with anyone? Sir Paul McCartney said it best: "If slaughterhouses had glass walls, everyone would be vegetarian."

We have been conditioned to separate the living, breathing sentient being who was simply wanting to enjoy his or her life from the hamburger or bacon on our plate. It has been proven that children are not born trying to eat animals. If you put a bunny in the crib with a baby, that baby would only want to play with the bunny! Even if the baby were hungry, the baby would not have the natural instincts to take a big bite of the sweet bunny. My passion regarding animals makes some people uncomfortable. I find it ironic that the ones who enjoy chawing on a leg or wing that previously belonged to a chicken find me the weird one! I invite you to try this experiment the next time you are enjoying a steak or pork chop. Tune in to what this animal looked like. Imagine his or her personality and if they had a family. I can promise you this: all animals have personalities and souls. Every last one of them.

I recall one goat I spoke with that was lucky enough to have been rescued and taken to an animal sanctuary. This goat told me that he knew he had been saved from slaughter. He fondly spoke of the ride to freedom when he was on his way to his new home, the sanctuary. The tour guide started laughing when I explained that this goat was showing me that it brings him tremendous joy to play tricks on everyone! In fact, he called himself the jokester of his group of farm animals. As the woman continued laughing, she revealed that he had learned how to unlatch the gate to let all the animals out, and that the sanctuary volunteers did call him a trickster. I would like to extend a personal thank you to Animal Haven of Asheville, where founders Barbara and Trina have been rescuing animals and farm animals for many years.

On another occasion, I was visiting a different animal sanctuary and had asked the owner not to give me any of the animals' names or tell me anything about them. As we were walking along, we happened upon one of the rescued pigs. I busted out laughing at what this pig relayed to me. He was quite serious when he haughtily informed me, "I am royalty, and I wear my crown with pride!" This pig literally showed me a crown on top of his head! The owner was astounded at what the pig had told me. He then explained that the pig's name was Sir Lancelot, and that they affectionately referred to him as their royal pig.

One time a client called me saying she was in serious need of help as her dog refused to be nice to her new fiancé who had just moved in with her. As I connected with the dog, I asked him why he didn't like the fiancé. The dog's frank reply:

"Because he stinks." I have been in some precarious situations with certain readings, but this one takes the cake! How could I possibly tell this woman who'd just paid me for a reading that her dog was offended by her fiancé's odor? I decided to just be honest and relay the information to her. Laughing hysterically, she admitted that her fiancé doused himself daily in potent cologne. I asked her if she would lovingly ask her beloved to be sparing with his cologne. After all,, this was truly disturbing her fur baby. She wholeheartedly agreed to ask him to make this grooming change! I then told the pup that we would handle the situation with the odor, but was there anything else he wanted to say to his mom? The sweet dog then said to me, "I had her all to myself for so long and then this big guy started coming around and then he never left. I felt sad that Mom was giving some of my attention to this big guy who smells funny." I bartered with the dog. I asked if he would be willing to start being nice to the big guy if the big guy changed his cologne or better yet, stopped wearing it altogether? The dog felt that was a good start. I showed him that if he could be nicer to the big guy, he could get love from two people instead of just one. I'm hopeful that a happy ending followed for this couple and their aroma-challenged pup.

Another memorable animal reading, this one over the phone, involved a cat in New York City. The cat told me that he had shared a past life with his mom, but in that life he was not a cat but rather a horse. The cat told me he missed being a horse. The owner was shocked when she explained that she had a saddle in her living room as a decoration and that the saddle was the cat's favorite place to hang out! This cat's guardian was Alicia Bowling of Creative Laughter Productions. After this reading, Alicia signed me to a contract to be involved in some of her metaphysical television shows she had written. Alicia's soul contract is to bring metaphysical awareness to the mainstream thru television shows. Plus, like Shay, Alicia is a huge animal lover, which is a super plus in my eyes!

There is one instance that still leaves me shocked. Many years ago, when I was still living in California, I found a baby sparrow outside that had fallen from his nest. I brought the baby bird inside and began dropper-feeding. In the beginning, I kept the bird in a makeshift nest made from a box and pine needles. As the days went by, the bird grew stronger and stronger. I kept him in a guest bedroom downstairs, away from the cats and dogs. When the bird was ready to learn to fly, I brought in an artificial tree for him to perch on. My friend eventually began to fly around the room, a glorious sight that only strengthened my deep bond with this sweet creature. With great sadness, I knew the time was drawing near for his release back out into the wild. There was a tree directly outside the window of the room where my sparrow had been raised. I took him outside and perched him on one of the branches. He was nervous at first but then bravely flew around the yard and came back. This routine went on for a few days as I continued to feed him from the tree outside and he became acclimated to his natural surroundings. After the third day, the bird flew off and did not return. I had such mixed emotions! I missed the sparrow terribly, but I knew his purpose did not include being trapped inside my home. One day about a year later, my stepson Austin told me there was a bird sitting on the top window ledge hitting the window with his beak. Honestly, it did not register with me until the third day the bird was outside the window. I thought, this bird can't possibly be the sparrow I raised and released, could it? I recalled it had been a little over a year since we had parted ways. Excitedly I stepped outside and looked up at the bird standing on a ledge of the upstairs window. Yes, this was a sparrow. Telepathically, I said to the bird, *If you are the bird I raised in my home, fly down beside me.* The bird then flew to the fence next to me. As I looked into his eyes, he telepathically communicated to me, *I just wanted to come back and thank you for saving my life.* We had a moment and then the bird flew off, never to return. As tears streamed down my face, I knew I had witnessed a miracle. I also knew in that moment that animals do have memories, feelings, and emotions. They have the capacity to feel gratitude and joy. Animals are here to teach us unconditional love.

Thank you for allowing me to get sidetracked from raving about *Best American Psychics!* But who doesn't adore cute animal stories?

A huge added bonus from being accepted into *Best American Psychics* is the soul tribe one immediately becomes part of. A soul tribe consists of a group of people who completely understand the essence of everyone in the group. Members generally share very similar beliefs, skills, and philosophies, along with a resonance of spirit. We are all there for one another. We provide comfort and understanding when one in the group is feeling more out of sorts or out of place than normal. We trade readings and help one another along our path. We celebrate our individual accomplishments. I can't begin to explain the sense of peace a person feels when among a group of colleagues who believe in you and have your best interests at heart. Some of my closest friends I met through *Best American Psychics*.

One of the first members I met was Allison Hayes, better known as The Rock Girl. Allison had won the Psychic of the Year Award for 2011 and 2012. She's an amazing spiritual teacher, motivational speaker, and an incredibly talented psychic. One of my favorite memories of Allison is when my mom took her Stones and Crystals class. Mom raved about what a stimulating teacher Allison is and how much she enjoyed the class. I was deeply honored to be a speaker alongside Allison on the 2017 Intuition Cruise. What an unbelievable journey that was! Allison now travels the world teaching her signature spiritual classes.

I met Kathy Biehl at one of the annual *Best American Psychics* retreats. Kathy is a long-standing member of the group, having won such honors as the Awesome Accolades Award. Kathy is one of the most well-rounded people I have ever met. She is an attorney, an actor, an astrologer, a writer, and a remarkable psychic. And she is great at all of these endeavors! Plus, she is super funny to boot. Kathy is a superb astrologer. She used her astrology expertise to help me choose the launch date for this book. Everything is comprised of energy, and astrology is quite powerful when someone is as knowledgeable as Kathy is.

Katherine Glass, who won Psychic of the Year for 2013 and 2019, is also someone I have connected with over the years. She and I took the same Advanced Mediumship course with Minister Colin Bates and Mavis Pittilla at Janet Nohavec's Spiritual Center, The Journey Within. We were roommates during this intensive weeklong course and had a blast together. Katherine invited me to join her and her husband at their healing Center in Boston for a mediumship gallery demonstration. My trip to the Healing Essence Center outside of Boston was a wonderful experience! Katherine and her husband Jonathan have created a beautiful space for healing to occur. Katherine is an awesome medium and it was a joy to serve the Spirit World with her.

I recommended that my friend and colleague Sally Rice apply for membership at *Best American Psychics*. Sally is one of the first professional psychics that I instantly became friends with. We met at a psychic fair in Ojai, California, and connected on the spot. I remember fondly that we both simultaneously received the message that the time had come for us to leave California. I was guided to move to Asheville, NC, and Sally was guided to move to Costa Rica, where she still resides. Sally reads for people all over the world and spends her free time biking, hiking, and swimming in the crystal blue waters of Costa Rica. Sally is an unbelievable manifestor. Just look at the life she has sculpted for herself and you will surely agree with me! Sally teaches workshops on manifesting and has taught me how to manifest many things.

One of my proudest moments came when one of my students, Anthony Mikolojeski, applied for membership and was accepted! Anthony is also known as The Asheville Medium. When Anthony came to see me years ago for a reading, his Spirit Guides exclaimed, "You are meant to be doing the same work that Jill is!" Anthony chuckled and admitted that a very well-known medium had given him the exact same message many years before this reading. I laughed and said, "And why is it you didn't listen to her all those years ago?" Anthony registered for my classes and began the journey into his true-life path and purpose. He then went on to study with other mediums, just as I had. It was an especially proud moment in my life and career when Anthony received his BAP (Best American Psychics) wings.

One way I have chosen to give back over the years is to offer my services pro bono as a psychic detective or psychic investigator. I discuss this more later in the book. I was led to create a group of colleagues to help with especially complex investigations. After a time at the helm, I passed the leadership baton over to Rebecca Pfeffer. I want to personally thank each member of this group for tirelessly offering their psychic expertise to the cold and unsolved cases that were brought to us. These professional psychics and mediums are not only amazing at what they do, they have hearts of gold. Our group of psychic sleuths included Amy Weidmann, Anthony Mikolojeski, Becky Pfeffer, Deborah Livingston, Kathy Biehl, Karen Lagace, Marc Lainhart, Sally Rice, Sara Beaupre, and Sharon Pugh.

There are fewer than 100 members of *Best American Psychics*. This will help you understand what an exclusive membership this is and what an honor it is to be listed among its members.

I consider each of these professionals to be colleagues, friends, and members of my Soul Tribe. For mediums, it feels especially rewarding when we find our Tribe. Why is this? Because finding our Tribe means we have found peeps who understand us. They are like us. Psychics and mediums generally feel very different, much like the purple elephant in the room. When we join forces with our Tribe, we feel much less lonely. We take comfort in the reality that there are others just like us who have been misunderstood their entire lives too. And with this knowledge comes a sense of peace, serenity, and warmth.

If you have not found your Soul Tribe yet, I encourage you to immediately put out your feelers for your Tribe. It's not unusual for our Soul Tribe to end up being closer to us than our biological family. It becomes easier to find your Tribe when you know what your life purpose is. A key component in raising our vibrational frequency and expanding our consciousness is recognizing that we are much more powerful united than separate. The days of the Me Generation are long gone. We are now in a time of realization, a time of synergy, as like minds joined together make it easier to weave the threads of our creations into a grander masterpiece. This is not only for our own personal evolution, but for the greater good of all. When we find our support system and Soul Tribe, and boldly walk together in sacred harmony, our personal magic radiates and intensifies tenfold.

Set the intention to find your Tribe. Ask and you shall receive. One of the most important things I have learned along my own spiritual journey is to surrender to Divine Will. When we surrender and begin to pay attention to the signs the Spirit World is giving us, the puzzle pieces of our life begin to miraculously fit together. Send out the energy and intention of Unity. Imagine instead yourself, sitting by a campfire with members of your Tribe. Take a moment to look around and truly experience the gratitude that you feel for your Tribe to be surrounding you. Revel in the security and intimacy you feel when you are together with members of your sacred sanctuary. This, my friends, is one of the secrets Sally Rice taught me in manifesting. *Don't wish it, be it.* Our thoughts create our reality.

When you find your Soul Tribe, they should want to see you succeed. They should be the wind beneath your angel wings, as you spread them and fly. The frequency of the fifth dimension is not about competition; it is about cooperation and collaboration. When we compete with another, it sends out the clear message of lack. Our Universe revolves on track, not lack. There is infinite abundance for us all. Your

Soul Tribe will remind you of your life purpose and offer support and guidance when needed.

In 2015, I was visiting my dad when I found out that I had been awarded the amazing Psychic of the Year Award! I cried happy tears as I told him about the accolade that had just been bestowed on me. Dad had tears in his eyes too as he congratulated me. I knew that night that it was no coincidence I was spending the night at Dad's house when I learned of my award. After all, he had been my greatest fan and most ardent supporter, the one who had encouraged me to honor my gifts on a professional basis. My cup of gratitude overflowed as I shared that thrilling honor with him. Considering the stunning talent and gifts of my *Best American Psychics* colleagues, I was humbled beyond belief. Then to my astonishment, I was again awarded the Psychic of the Year Award in 2016.

I owe unending depths of gratitude to Shay and her sister Angel for manning the decks of *Best American Psychics* every day. BAP has not only changed my life but gifted me with a support group of individuals I would never have had the pleasure of knowing. *Best American Psychics* tirelessly disseminates the proof that the paranormal is actually normal -- and increasingly recognized as such. It lends professionalism to an industry that was previously misunderstood. And *Best American Psychics* furnishes a forum for each member to continue to strive for excellence in their craft.

Shay Parker, thank you for answering the call to your soul purpose. You have played a huge role in helping to shape my life as I navigated my own soul purpose. You have laid the foundation of a sacred space where a group of eccentrics can find their Tribe. And you have created a registry where people may find a psychic or medium, confidently knowing that each professional listed is ethical, accurate, and tested.

I am super proud to be BAP-approved!

Chapter 5

Stranger Things

I knew I could not complete this book without a chapter on many of the bizarre events that have happened in my life. Even though I am a medium and my entire life is strange, some of these events even had me questioning my reality. If you are a skeptical type of person, you may understandably question the authenticity of some of the experiences that have shaped my life. All I can do is relay these events just as I lived them, with truth, honesty, and full integrity. It is up to you to see how and whether the reality of these experiences fits into your own reality.

One reason I have been guided to share these events is to remind everyone how amazing and powerful we are. We are all out-of-this-world extraordinary. It is time to remember the exceptional gifts we each have come to share. Your gifts may have come in a different package than mine; however, I promise that you have something unique and special to offer. Once you recognize and realize the gifts you brought with you into this lifetime, the puzzle pieces of your life begin to merge together beautifully.

UFO

There is a great deal of controversy about whether aliens exist or not. I know they are real because I saw one when I was a child. My parents were in Europe and my sister and I and our cousins who lived next door were outside playing. Suddenly, we looked up, and across the street from us was a very large cylindrical object hovering over the neighbor's roof. The craft was changing colors rapidly. One of my cousins ran inside to get his mother. When my aunt and Granny, the woman who was staying with us, came outside and saw the craft, they made us go inside, as they were quite afraid. I was totally bummed out because I was not afraid of this ship, or whatever it was, at all! In fact, I was mesmerized. By the time I ran inside and up to my room to look out the window, it was gone. There have been quite a few sightings in Mississippi. For some reason, this seems to be a hot spot of activity.

Over the years, I have spotted spacecraft in the sky quite often. There have even been times when I was able to telepathically communicate with the ships. I know I have been abducted, but have no recollection of the actual event. It's just something I have a knowing about. I also have the "scoop" on my shin, which is a tell-tale sign you have been abducted. When I lived in Sedona, Arizona, I would watch the craft every night. It fascinated me to think about their technology, their day-to-day lives, and how much more advanced they are than we.

There will be full disclosure one day soon. I see this happening sooner rather than later. Our government has known about aliens and other nonhuman life for many years. In fact, it is my belief that some of our top officials have been in contact with them. There is nothing to fear from other life forms. If our government ever tries to instill fear of extraterrestrials, do not fall victim to this trap. Trust me, if these advanced beings wished to harm us, they would already have done so. Most of them are doing their best to save us from ourselves, protecting us from the misuse of potentially harmful nuclear technologies

I look forward to the day of full disclosure. I honestly feel this is closer than ever to being part of our known reality. This expanded knowledge will go a long way in raising the awareness of many people on our planet.

Anthony Lombardi

Tony Lombardi was shot and killed on September 16, 2008. A year or so later, the Los Angeles County Sheriff's Department had an article published in the Santa Clarita Valley Signal newspaper asking for the public's help since the case was still unsolved. My friend Joan, who was an acquaintance of Mr. Lombardi's family, saw the article and called me to see if I would psychically tune in and see if I could get anything. I was not familiar with the case but told Joan I would happily try to connect with Tony in the Spirit World and see what I could discover.

What I got was a lot! Tony told me exactly what happened and who had arranged his murder. He told me he had recently helped a woman who had fallen on hard times. Tony gave me her name. He had allowed her to temporarily move in with him. He went on to tell me that she knew his schedule and that she had him murdered to gain money she knew he had on him. Tony explained that she had not been the one to pull the trigger; however, she had arranged for others to do it. Tony said that two men pulled up to his car and shot him point-blank in the middle of the day. I don't remember all the exact details he gave me about the men, but I do remember the name he gave me because of what transpired next.

The article gave the detective's name and phone number and said if anyone had any information on this case to please call. My initial voicemail message went like this: "Hi, my name is Jill and I'm a psychic medium with information on the murder of Tony Lombardi. Here's my phone number. I look forward to hearing back from you."

Days went by in silence, with no returned phone call. I thought, this is so strange. Maybe they want help from anyone and everyone except if you happen to be a psychic medium. So, I tried another angle. I called back and said, "My name is Elizabeth and I have information on the murder of Tony Lombardi." Hours later my phone rang with the detective, eager to hear my info. After I got him on the line, I admitted that Elizabeth was my middle name and that I had called days before, offering assistance. I asked if he had received my message. He then went on to inform me that he didn't need any help from psychics. My devil horns shot up as I slyly asked how it was working out for him, trying to solve the case on his own without the help of psychics. He agreed to meet with me.

I walked into the sheriff's station the next day with my channeled notes in hand. At first he said he needed to "test" me and that I could give him a reading so that he could believe in my gifts. "Tell me something you would have no way of knowing," he challenged. I looked at this detective and said, "Sir, I have better things to do with my time than to sit here and entertain you. I am doing this out of the goodness of my heart, simply trying to help. I have nothing to gain by sitting here with you today. A friend asked me to help so here I am, helping. Do you want to know what I got or not?"

I then told him the woman's name who had arranged the murder. I explained that Tony told me he had tried to help this woman. The detective looked at me and said, "Yes, she is our main suspect, but you could have learned this detail from the family." Highly annoyed by now, I told him I'd had no contact with the family, or anyone connected with this case. I went on to tell him how he could get his suspect to "sing". He took a few notes and thanked me for my time. I knew he would choose to ignore the information I had given.

I called my friend Joan and recounted how the meeting had not gone well. I then offered to meet with the family of Tony and give them a free reading to help bring them some closure. Later that week, I met with some of Tony's family members on a beautiful sunny day in California and brought their father through with much validating evidence and many personal messages. During that session, they told me they had never liked or trusted this woman and that they tried to warn their dad -- to no avail. Their father was a good soul who loved helping people. During this exchange, they told him they were going to contact the suspect themselves, but he asked them not to, as exposure to the people she was involved with would be too dangerous.

I found another article, written in 2011, that claimed the Santa Clarita Valley Sheriff's Office had even received tips from psychics that did not help. According to the article: "'We were skeptical,' Loman recalled. 'We got these GPS coordinates, but you think it would be easier to get the name (of a suspect).'" If you had been in the room with me when I read this article, you would have heard me screaming quite loudly. I DID give them the name of the suspect, but they were not interested in handling the case the way I advised them to.

To this day, this murder remains unsolved and the killers are roaming free.

Thankfully, there are more and more detectives open to working with psychics and mediums. We are mediums, not detectives. We are not trying to be detectives. What we can do is channel information and details which have been known to help solve crimes. It is my hope that all police departments will eventually have a department for psychic sensitives.

Michael Jackson

I am writing this section on the ten-year anniversary of Michael Jackson's passing. Like many, I grew up singing and dancing to Michael's music. It was 2009 and I had left Southern California to move outside of Sedona, Arizona. One night shortly after the icon's death, I was woken up suddenly. This was not unusual for me as many spirits attempt to get my attention while I am sleeping. What was unusual was that Michael Jackson was standing in my room. He telepathically communicated to me that he'd been murdered. He told me that Dr. Murray had murdered him, and that he was not working alone. There were others involved. Michael was distraught, explaining to me that he never would have left his children as they were his world. He went on to tell me that he was innocent of the sinister claims of sexual abuse that had been levelled against him. He needed to be assured that the truth would eventually come out. He wanted to reach out to mediums the world over who could possibly help him.

I was shaken to my core. I prayed and meditated on this for days. I asked my Spirit Guides if it would be proper for me to contact Michael's family at that time. I was told no. They were in shock and enduring a living hell. It was not the time. I'd certainly not want to cause them further distress, as they had no idea who I was or why Michael would have contacted me. I was told to patiently wait, and I would know when the time was right to publicly reveal Michael's words to me.

I shared the visitation with my family, friends, and some of my colleagues. In the years that followed, whenever anyone tried to badmouth Michael, I would stand up for his honor and explain his innocence.

Fast-forward ten years. It was early 2019, and I was at Soul Synergy Center. In walks, a beautiful lightworker who introduced herself to me as Iman Ali. Iman explained that she was a Reiki Master Teacher, psychic, and medium who had been living in Chicago. But something had called her back home to Mississippi. She wondered how she could possibly share her gifts in the Bible Belt, but she had listened to her guidance and moved back to Mississippi. She started searching for a spiritual New Age center, thinking such an entity probably did not exist in Mississippi. She then found Soul Synergy Center and excitedly drove over to check us out. Iman later said she is not sure what propelled her to talk about Michael Jackson, but that she was led to. In the first few minutes of meeting me, she explained that while working on a project with him, she had received the message that he was in danger. I stopped her in the middle of her story, exclaiming, "You are not going to believe this, but Michael Jackson visited me shortly after his death." "Me too!" she shot back. We began sharing the messages with each other that Michael shared with us. I still get chills when I think about this. There are no accidents in this world! Everything is connected and everything happens for a reason!

Stop for a moment and consider the magnitude of what happened here. A white medium (me) living in Sedona, Arizona, was contacted by Michael Jackson. Around the same time, a black medium (Iman) living in New York City was also contacted by Michael. Ten years later they both find themselves living in the Bible Belt of Mississippi and meet at a Spiritual Center. The two then experience the instant rapport of spiritual connection.

We began trading readings with each other. With each reading and healing, more magic occurred for both of us. Michael had been connecting with Iman over the years, and after Iman and I met, he began giving me messages again too. One day he continuously played the song "Black or White" in my head. He told me, "It is no accident that a white medium and a black medium have joined together in the Deep South." He went on to say, "You were brought together to help heal traumas from the past and to build bridges to the future." Tears are streaming down my face as I allow these powerful words to sink deeply into my heart.

The night of the ten-year anniversary, Iman and I and two of my students got together to connect with Michael. The experience was incredible! Iman channeled Michael as a direct voice medium that night. A direct voice medium is a medium who allows the loved one to "borrow" their physical body and speak through them. After Iman completed her session, I in turn channeled Michael's father as a direct voice medium. Two other group consciousness federations were also channeled through me that evening to give us beautiful messages about what is to come, and the part Iman is meant to play in bringing truth about the proper honor and legacy of Michael Jackson.

Michael was a channel, his music channeled from other realms. He was a pure angel. He was also extremely intelligent, yet innocent and trusting in many ways. Michael has told Iman and me that he is thrilled to be helping us both from the Other Side. I am honored and humbled beyond words. Iman is writing a book about her experiences with this amazing man who was such a gift to our world.

Michael, thank you for the beautiful Light you were and continue to be to our world. Some would say rest in peace, but I know you are not resting, Michael. You are still shining your bright Light and doing your best to help heal our world.

Mitrice Richardson

The year was 2009, and a beautiful young woman named Mitrice went missing from Malibu, California. I was not familiar with the case until Mitrice woke me up one night to ask for my help. I was sleeping soundly when someone in the Spirit World made themselves known so I would wake up. When I opened my eyes, Mitrice was standing at the foot of my bed. She spoke to me telepathically and asked me for my help. She explained that she had been murdered and needed me to contact her dad. She then showed me one of the men responsible by creating a holographic image of him on the side of my bed. This was a first for me! I had someone from the Spirit World in my bedroom *and* a holographic image of a murderer who was still alive at the side of my bed! I assured Mitrice that I would do my best to help her.

The next morning, searching online for a way to contact Mitrice's father, I was able to locate his name and email address. I proceeded to email Michael Richardson, explaining that I am a medium and what had transpired in my room the previous night. I told him that even though I am a professional medium, I would help him pro bono. He immediately wrote me back saying he would really appreciate my help. I asked him to bring some items of her clothing with him so I could feel her energy better. This is called psychometry, when a psychic or medium holds and receives impressions from an object. All things hold energetic imprints and can sometimes be an aid in connecting more easily.

We agreed to meet at a restaurant in Los Angeles. I immediately made the connection to Mitrice and channeled information to her dad for about two hours. For my own safety, I am not going to relay some of the particulars given to me. Let's just put it this way: justice has not been served in this case, and the multiple people responsible for this horrific murder are not behind bars. After I finished communicating with Mitrice, I told Michael that for many reasons, it would be years before the killers would be brought to justice, but that he would be able to successfully bring suit against the Malibu Police Department. In 2011, my prediction came true, as Michael Richardson and Los Angeles County reached a settlement in the matter. I can assure you that this monetary settlement does nothing to ease the trauma of what his entire family has endured.

For those of you unfamiliar with this tragic case, Richardson had been arrested at a popular restaurant on the Pacific Coast Highway in Malibu. When Mitrice was in the restaurant, she seemed to be behaving in an erratic manner. She was unable to pay her bill, so the restaurant staff called the police. The Los Angeles County sheriff's deputies towed her car and took her to the Malibu/Lost Hills Sheriff's station. Mitrice's mother called the station that evening to make sure her daughter was not going to be released that night since she was a long way from home. She was assured that her daughter would not be released that night. Yet at 12:38 a.m., without money or a phone, Mitrice was released into the night. Did the police really expect this young girl to hike the 11 miles to where her car had been towed? It's interesting to note that in 2006 when Mel Gibson was arrested and transported to this same Malibu/ Lost Hills station, he was privately escorted to his towed car after he was released. Let's see if we can quickly sum up what the differences are here. Mitrice was not famous, and Mel Gibson was not a young black girl. It does not take a psychic to figure this one out.

It is interesting to note that at first Captain Thomas Martin of the department claimed there was no video footage of Mitrice exiting the police station at almost 1:00 a.m. Yet miraculously, five months later, Captain Martin suddenly found the tape and claimed it had been sitting there on his desk right along. Apparently, the tape shows a deputy leaving the station shortly after Mitrice walked out. This is one thing that Mitrice did show me that night she appeared in my bedroom. The deputy first lied about being at Lost Hills when Mitrice was there and then later claimed he did nothing wrong.

One other thread of synchronicity in my experiences is something Mitrice reportedly said that night when she was at the restaurant in Malibu. Someone claims Mitrice said she was wanting to avenge Michael Jackson's death. Is it coincidence that Mitrice Richardson and Michael Jackson both contacted me after their transition to the Other Side? I think not.

My hope and prayer is that one day soon the group of men responsible for this lovely young woman's death will face justice. It is also my quest to continue to promote awareness of the fact that *much* of the time black people are still treated very differently than white people when it comes to law enforcement. If Mitrice Richardson had been a young white woman of affluence or fame, she would not have been arrested, she would not have been released into the dark of the night to walk 11 miles on her own, and she would not have been brutally murdered.

Mitrice will always hold a special place in my heart. I sincerely wish we had met under different circumstances. It was a beautiful honor to connect Michael Richardson with his angel in heaven.

Florida Doctor

From time to time I travel to Florida to do private sittings, teach, and offer public mediumship demonstrations. My assistant always books my sessions, so I don't even pay attention to the names on the list until the day of the appointments when I jot down the names and times of each person coming to see me that day. At the time of this event, my mom Gail was my assistant. It is my policy that a second party may not schedule an appointment for someone else. This is for many reasons, but first and foremost, if someone forces or pressures a loved one to visit a medium and they are not ready, the session will not go well for anyone involved. Therefore, my policy is that each individual schedule his or her private session themselves. My mom received a request from a mother who wanted to schedule and pay for a session for herself and a separate one for her son. Mom explained to the lady that her son must call to schedule the private session himself, and that if she wanted to pay for her son's session, she could do that. The woman insisted that her son was on board with everything, explaining that her daughter-in-law had been murdered and they needed to connect with her. Touched, Mom made an exception for her. (For the privacy of these clients, I am going to refer to this woman as Beth.) Mom always called everyone the day before to remind them of their appointment time. After she got off the phone, Mom had a very strange feeling that I was not to do this reading. She called me and told me she felt I was to cancel the reading. Mom then revealed that Beth had confided that her son was a suspect in the murder of his wife. For readings, I choose not to know anything about anyone. However, I decided to move forward with the reading as planned, and asked Mom not to share any other information with me that Beth may have provided.

That night I was on a Skype call with my friend and colleague, psychic medium Sally Rice. I was telling her about the strange feeling Mom had about me going forward with a reading I'd be doing the next day. I told Sally I had a private session scheduled with a mother, followed by a session with her son, and that the son was a suspect in his wife's murder. The purpose was for me to connect with the deceased, who would reveal who murdered her. Just then, Sally exclaimed, "Jill, there is a woman sitting behind you on the kitchen counter!" Now mind you, I was in this vacation rental by myself. I then looked at the reflection via Skype and I saw her too! To validate what we were both seeing, we described to the other what she looked like and what she was wearing. She then started communicating with both of us. She told us that she was the woman who had been murdered and that her husband was the one who had murdered her. I asked her why in the world would her husband want to come in for a session with me if he is the murderer? She explained that he was a skeptic and was coming to me only because his mother was forcing him to. I assured her that I would not be reading for her husband, who had hired someone to take her life, leaving their children without a mother. At that point, I looked online to see if the woman who was sitting in my kitchen was indeed the same woman who had been murdered. She was.

As you can imagine, I got very little sleep that night. This was a first for me! I had no intention of sharing space with someone who had killed his wife. The next morning, I contacted Beth and explained to her that I would be refunding her money because I was not going forward with the reading. She argued with me, saying that she had waited many months for this reading. I apologized and told her that my Guides had instructed me not to conduct the session. I refunded her money. A few months later, her son was arrested and charged with murder for hire in the death of his wife.

One of my students in Florida asked if she could talk to me about something that was quite upsetting to her. When I sat down with her, she explained that the woman who had been killed had come to her and told her that her husband was the one who had orchestrated her murder. My student had been a patient of the woman, who was a doctor. She asked me if she should go to the authorities. I advised   that it had to be her call, but that police departments generally do not give much credence to a dream or a vision about a crime. While more and more police agencies are using psychic detectives, there is always the frustrating possibility that a psychic medium just trying to help out will be disregarded.

This was a very difficult situation for me. My heart was broken over what this woman had gone through and what her children were having to endure. My prayers and condolences continue to go out to her family and other loved ones. It is some comfort to know that she is still able to communicate with her daughters and is one of their guardian angels in heaven.

This is a valuable lesson in listening to our guidance. I also know it is no coincidence that I was on a Skype video call with Sally that evening. I have no doubt the wife would have done everything necessary to get my attention. However, witnessing what I witnessed with Sally was one of those out of this world crazy moments of my life.

John Lennon

One day I was sitting on my yoga mat in our Healing Center, excitedly looking forward to the weekend as I'd be teaching Level 2 Mediumship to a wonderful group of students. Suddenly, my gaze fell to the hardwood floor -- and there was a face in the floor. You would think that by this point in my life I would be used to such things! Yet, I closed my eyes and shook my head to clear it, lest I simply be "seeing things." Reopening my eyes, I looked again. Yep, the face was still there. Tuning in to whatever or whomever it might be, I noticed round glasses on the man's face. It hit me like the proverbial ton of bricks: John Lennon's face was staring back at me! I was as giddy as a schoolgirl with her first crush. I had briefly made a connection to John Lennon a few years back, as one of my friends and colleagues has a strong spiritual connection to him and has connected with him as well. And here he was now, in my yoga room, peering out at me through those little round spectacles! I didn't have time to fully connect to his energy and see what he was doing there that day. After all, I was teaching a mediumship course that weekend so I figured he must have shown up to offer his support for the class. I felt him all weekend as I was teaching. but I didn't have time to blend with him and find out if there was another reason for his presence. It was Iman who finally offered clarity on the matter.

John Lennon is another piece in the puzzle of why musicians who were murdered are drawn to psychics like me. Sadly, this is a reality we must face. Most famous musicians are extremely gifted. Many freely admit that the music they write is channeled from higher dimensions. Often, they become too powerful and have too much influence over the masses. Therefore, there are some people of power that see to it that they are murdered. John Lennon has made it known that he is working with me as well as with other mediums to wake people up to the deep corruption that is still going on in our society. What a humbling and thrilling experience to have the soul of John Lennon helping me with my work!

And lately, Iman and I have both been visited by other recently murdered musicians. She and I know we are to work together to bring awareness and closure to these senseless crimes.

Many people have not given enough credence to the power of music and lyrics. I have discussed energy and vibration throughout the book. I invite you to sit and ponder about why certain musicians met the same fate in their lives. Do your best to think for yourselves and not fall into the trap of the masses led by mainstream media.

I have no doubt that this chapter will be met with no small amount of skepticism. Honestly, I don't blame skeptics. After all, if someone started chatting with me in a grocery line about their conversations with Michael Jackson, as well as some recent schmoozing with John Lennon, I would probably just nod my head and smile politely as I gathered my bags and bolted for the door! In all seriousness, I think about how many people have been locked up in insane asylums who were simply mediums who didn't know how to handle their gifts. I feel very thankful and blessed that I can freely talk and write about my experiences without being placed in a straitjacket.

So, if someone wants to laugh or remain skeptical about whether these phenomena actually occurred, more power to them. In all honesty, it's still a bit jarring to me when I go back and relive these bizarre events. I can't tell you how amusing it is to me when someone who's about to relay a strange story to me starts with, "You may think I'm strange for what I'm about to say." My response is always the same -- "Girl ...please!"

Chapter 6
My Twin Flame

As I mentioned earlier, I have had quite a few "learning and soul growth opportunities" when it comes to my love life. Most of them were karmic past-life relationships that we had agreed to balance in this lifetime. Some were simply screwups on my part and not listening to my better judgement!

After Austin's father and I split up, I was single for five years. I needed that time to myself to continue my spiritual work. I have found it to be true that most of the time, we will not meet our twin flame before we have done our personal work. We meet plenty of soul mates along the way; however, twin flames are different.

What is the difference between a soul mate and a twin flame? We have only one twin flame. And most of the time we choose not to incarnate with our twin flame. Normally, the other half of the twin stays behind, so to speak, to help the other twin from the Other Side. I have noticed an escalation of twin flames incarnating together and uniting during these times. We are living in very special times, pivotal times in our planet's evolution. What I have personally found is that when twin flames do incarnate together, it is to work as a team in some capacity. When I say work, it doesn't have to be a physical nine-to-five job. The twins may end up volunteering in some way or creating a company that helps shift the consciousness of millions of people. Maybe they are both artisans, or creative in a way that supports the other twin on their path. What I mean is that there is a very special purpose to their union that is not only for their personal benefit but for the good of many. Traditionally, a soul mate is for the explicit benefit of the two people involved in that union. Soul mates come together by soul contract agreement and have normally shared at least one past life together. The past life or lives may not have been on planet Earth, but they have shared incarnations together in the past.

Part of the soul contract my husband Daniel and I had was to create a spiritual healing New Age center in the deep Bible Belt of Mississippi. We didn't realize this for some time after we met; however, our souls had agreed to it before we were born. I will talk about our center, Soul Synergy Center, later on in the book as it is one of the accomplishments I am most proud of.

About a year before I met Daniel, my psychic medium friend and colleague Leanna Marino predicted him. She explained that she had "seen" my twin flame coming into my life. She told me his name would begin with a D, that he would be just a tad under 6' tall, his eyes would look like mine, he would be younger than me, we would meet in a bar, and that he would love shoes! She also said that she saw his hair in a ponytail. One fateful night in September I was supposed to meet friends for a play and then go have a glass of wine at the wine bar. The friends cancelled last minute, and I almost didn't go. However, something told me to go anyway. I had never gone to a play by myself. Yet something urged me to be courageous and go alone. Halfway through the play I decided to leave because it wasn't that great. Just as I was about to head home, a little voice said go have one glass of wine at the wine bar first. As I took my first sip of wine, Daniel walked in. As a side note, he was not supposed to be there that night either. He ended up stopping in last minute because of a change of plans. He got a glass of wine and walked over to me. He introduced himself as Daniel. We both admitted later that we both knew right away that we would never be without each other from that moment forward. As we continued to talk about everything imaginable, Daniel commented on how our eyes were the exact same color. We discovered that our eyes change color depending on our emotions. I found out that Daniel is 5'11" and 5 years younger than me. When he started talking about how much he loves shoes, I started laughing. I knew my life was forever changed that night.

Over the years, I continued to marvel at the precision of Leanna's prediction. However, there was one small detail she predicted that had not come to pass. She saw Daniel with a ponytail. I never told Daniel about this part of her prediction because I honestly thought she had seen this part incorrectly. I felt six out of seven "hits" was amazing enough. A few months ago, years after we met, Daniel said to me, "I have decided to let my hair grow out so I can have a ponytail." Again, I started laughing hysterically. Bingo! Seven out of seven, Leanna! If I haven't mentioned it yet, I have the most gifted and amazing colleagues.

Many people have the notion that the twin flame dynamic is rose-colored glasses, unicorns, and rainbows all the time, with a harp playing softly in the background. For the most part, this is simply not true. Before we expand on this topic further, I would like to first examine the differences between soul mates and twin flames.

We each have many soul mates in our lifetimes. Soul mates can be friends, siblings, a parent, lovers, a child, or even an animal. Soul mates are members of our soul groups, and we have shared past lives with these individuals. There is an instant bond or knowing recognition when soul mates lock eyes. Soul mates come into our lives to gently assist us along our path, many times creating a safe haven for us to explore our soul growth.

However, sometimes soul mates may enter our lives to simply balance karma from previous lifetimes. In my practice, I have found this to be the case primarily between lovers or couples. When this occurs, the union may not last the entire lifetime. When the karma is complete, one of the soul mates may choose to leave the union. If you feel you are in a karmic relationship from a past life, ask yourself if the karma is truly complete and if it is time to move on. So many people remain in relationships and partnerships with soul mates long after the karma has been balanced and is complete. This can prevent other soul mates from entering their lives. Many stay for security or because it feels safe. Yet, when we can be completely honest with ourselves, we clearly see that safety and security do not direct us to the path of our soul contracts.

We are each bound by soul contracts that we agreed to honor before we incarnated. Various soul mates from our immediate and neighboring soul groups have agreed to play particular roles in assisting us along the way to fulfilling these contracts. Some soul mates may serve as catalysts for us to swiftly alter our life and head in the appropriate direction of what we came here to accomplish. Each individual came to this Earth to express something unique. In addition to our own personal   opportunity for expansion, growth, and enlightenment, we have agreed to play some role in the expansion of the collective. Every role is important and necessary.

Sometimes soul mates enter our lives to properly prepare us for meeting our twin flame. For the most part, twin flames meet later in life, or even if they have met at an earlier age, they come together later when they are older. Each twin has their own individual work to accomplish prior to meeting their other half. Daniel and I have both commented that we would not have been ready for each other had we met when we were younger. One of the keys to a full and vibrant life is being present and aware of the roles various people are playing in our lives, and being honest with ourselves when it is time to move on. More than likely, you will connect with these individuals on the Other Side and/or in another lifetime. But again, remember that this is a free-will soul's choice. I chuckle as I recall some of my clients imploring, "Please tell me my lifetimes with this SOB are complete!" All joking aside, we do have the free will to decide on each lifetime and the role others will play in that life. Keep in mind that we have incarnated in a 3D reality. The Spiritual Law of Polarity is alive and well! We humans truly require the dark to fully appreciate the light. When we experience grief, we learn to love more deeply. Without the dark of the night, we would not experience the dawn of each new day. It is not an easy undertaking, but try to appreciate all experiences. When we reach the point where we can actually thank a soul mate – or even an outright antagonist -- for their assistance along our paths, our individual consciousness expands. It may feel odd or unnatural to thank someone for hurting us in some way, and to sincerely forgive them. Yet, when someone causes us pain, the experience teaches us what we will refuse to accept in the next beloved. We learn and grow from each relationship and each experience we have, both good and bad.

The twin flame dynamic is the most intense relationship you will ever have with another sentient being. The love will be the deepest and most profound. However, if we have not learned to love ourselves, and discovered that we must love ourselves first and foremost, the twin flame union cannot last. This may seem selfish to some people. But it's not selfish at all. Think about it this way: If we don't love and honor ourselves, and our twin flame is the other half of our soul, they will continue to mirror back to us a lack of love. This is a recipe for relationship disaster.

The role of the twin is to take us as far as we can go toward enlightenment. The twin flame often has a special talent for pushing our buttons. It can become a deep and intense power struggle. It can test you to the point of wanting to run away.

And many twins do run. For a while. The twin can't seem to stay away from the other twin for long. When a twin runs, it means they are not ready for the intensity of the twin flame union. This can be terribly painful for the twin left behind. Many times, the other twin knows and recognizes the other person to be their twin. It is important to remember, however, that even though we chose to incarnate with our twin flame, each twin has free will. Just because you are twins does not mean you will end up with the fairy-tale ending. Both twins must be ready for the intensity of this ride.

What I have witnessed with my own clients, my friends who are with their twin, and in my own personal twin flame relationship is this: The more personal work each individual has completed and the more they have learned to trust and surrender and stay out of ego, the easier the twin flame relationship is to navigate and sustain. The twin flame dynamic is meant to be the flowing and merging of energies in a beautiful dance of fire. When we have done our work, the fire ignites in passions and creativities that birth new realms of consciousness expansion for everyone involved. When we are still living in the cramped space of ego and control dynamics, the fire can all but consume us.

If you have not found your twin flame or even a long-lasting soul mate, I invite you to reflect on any areas in your life that could still use some tuning up (so to speak). Be honest with yourself. In our moments of true honesty and quiet contemplation, whirlwind flashes of inspiration and knowing may strike! Many times, over my years of doing readings, the timing has been off as to when my client would meet their twin or beloved soul mate. I can't tell you the number of times a client realized that they were simply not ready. This type of discernment has opened tremendous opportunities for their subsequent evolution.

I cringe when I hear a client say, "There are no good men out there." If you are engaging in this type of negative talk, please try to stop it now! Our thoughts and beliefs create our reality. If you constantly repeat the mantra, "There are no good men" all the time, trust me when I say this, you will attract all the "no good men!" If you desire to meet your soul contract beloved, it is important that you make your desires known to the Universe.

A couple of years before I met Daniel, I decided to get playful with my vision board. A vision board, for those who have never heard of this, is a visualization created with words and/or art on paper that represents your heart's desires. What we focus on expands. If you have never created a vision board, I encourage you to do so. Maybe you can find a workshop in your area that teaches the art of creating vision boards. It's a great deal of fun to engage in this project with others as the energy from the experience magnifies everyone's intentions. Some people cut out words or pictures from old magazines to paste on their vision board.

For my personal life partner vision board, I used construction paper and colorful markers. At the top of it I wrote: *Thank you, Universe, for bringing my beloved into my life. He is everything I had ever hoped for.* I wrote down all the qualities I desired in my life partner and put a star beside each one. An important one for me was this: *My beloved loves animals as much as I do and will embrace living with lots of them.* Another one was: *My beloved embraces and lovingly supports my gifts of Mediumship.* After I finished writing down all of my wishes and putting a star next to each one, I packed the paper away. When you do this, there is an energy of trust that goes along with it. I made my desires known to the Universe and now the Universe will deliver. After Daniel and I moved in together and I was unpacking one of my boxes, I came across my vision board sheet. I was ecstatic as I read each one and realized that Daniel had every single quality I had envisioned! I showed the paper to Daniel and sweetly explained to him that the Universe had created him for me from the love of my powerful vision board!

Since our thoughts, patterns, and beliefs create our reality, make sure your surroundings are welcoming to a life partner. You may want to find a Feng Shui expert to ensure that your home has the proper placements, so the energy will attract your mate. Rose quartz, rhodochrosite, garnet, emerald, moonstone and lapis lazuli are great crystals for calling love into your life. Meditate with these crystals as you imagine all the exciting things you and your love will enjoy together.

Journal about what your life purpose is. As mentioned earlier, we are more likely to meet our twin flame or soul mate when we are following our life's calling. Even if you and your twin flame have agreed not to incarnate together in this lifetime and your soul contract is to join with a soul mate you have spent many lifetimes with, it is best to be on the path of your purpose prior to calling in your mate. When we have stepped into the essence of who we are and what we came here to do, more opportunities appear for us to meet those of like mind. If your soul purpose is to rescue animals, would it not make sense for you to join in unity with another animal lover? Start attending events that resonate with your heart's desire.

New moon ceremonies can be quite powerful in releasing the old and igniting an energy of the new in our lives. I encourage you to find an astrologer whom you admire and resonate with and subscribe to their newsletters. They will update you on the moon cycles and how the planets will play out with each new moon.

Forgive your exes. Yes, you read this sentence correctly. If you are not ready to truly forgive your exes, you are not

113

ready for a sacred union. When we remain in victim mode and replay the story repeatedly of how so and so really "did a number on me," this is the energetic vibration we become stuck in. When you are in a lower vibrational frequency, this is not the space to attract soul mates and twin flames. I wince when I am conducting a reading for someone who is wanting to find true love and they are still focused on an ex. I will ask them in the session, "Have you forgiven your ex and performed a cord-cutting release ceremony with them?" Many times, my client will say, "Oh yes, absolutely! I did that the last new moon!" And then the next question from their mouth is, "Is my ex still thinking about me?" Or, "Is my ex going to stay with the new girlfriend?" Friends, when you have completely let go of someone and have forgiven and released them, you could care less if your name ever crosses their lips again. Further, you *want* them to find love and happiness with someone else. Be honest with yourself and admit when you have not energetically released someone from your past. A Reiki Master Healer or other energy healer can assist with this. Locate someone in your area who helps with cord-cutting and removing stuck and stagnant energy.

And by far the most important advice I can give to someone wishing to call in their true love is this: Make sure you love yourself more than anyone else in this world. This does not mean you go into egocentric mode and spend all day pampering yourself and admiring yourself in the mirror! What it does mean is that you begin a practice in which you wake up every day and hug yourself and tell yourself how much you love you! It's even powerful to thank your body for all it does for you. Practice dwelling in a space of joy and bliss. These emotions raise our vibrational frequency, which sends out signals to others who are vibrating on similar frequencies. Like attracts like. If you maintain a high frequency, you are much more likely to attract a divine partner who vibrates at a comparable frequency. Recognize that you and your beloved will join together for a soul purpose of learning from each other.

Daniel and I have taken turns being the teacher and being the student. It is egoic to think that one person in the relationship knows everything and the other is a perpetual student. He and I have learned to swiftly and flexibly change roles as the teacher and as the student. When there was struggle in our relationship, it was always over control. When we attempt to control another person, we are not allowing them the free will choice to make their own decisions. Very often, when we are exercising our ego in efforts to control, sway, or influence another, it is because we are stuck in a place of fear. The very nature of the twin flame union is to hold up a mirror to the other twin. When the mirrored twin is not standing in the power of their highest potential, conflict may arise.

The key is to learn to recognize what that damned mirror looks like! In the beginning, its reflections may come seemingly from out of nowhere, when you least expect it. Over time, if both twins are fully committed, that mirror increasingly reflects darker aspects of the person that have come out to play. If one of your shadows is staring back at you, take some time to honestly recognize what you are seeing. We all have a shadow side. It's when we learn to recognize and embrace our shadows that true healing and expansion occur.

What is the shadow? According to Carl Jung, the "shadow," "id," or "shadow aspect/archetype" may refer to (1) an unconscious aspect of the personality which the conscious ego does not identify in itself, or (2) the entirety of the unconscious, i.e., everything of which a person is not fully conscious. In short, the shadow is the unknown side. I highly recommend Caroline Myss's book, *Soul Contracts,* for further discussion of the shadow, archetypes, and life purpose direction. The shadow does not have to always be negative. It becomes negative when we don't recognize it or learn to work with the lessons it desires to teach us. Daniel has been my strongest teacher, as he has learned to hold my mirror steady and strong when I have needed it. And I have been able to do the same for him. During times of great challenge in our relationship we have both said that our union is destined, and there is no plan B. We will ride this incredible wave together, and if one of us falls off, the other has agreed to help the other climb back up.

For those of you who have joined with your twin flame or beloved soul mate, I encourage you to focus on the positive aspects of your mate's behaviors rather than the negative. We all have less than flattering aspects of ourselves or areas that could stand some improvement. If we understand that our words create a certain frequency, does it not make sense to speak only words of love and encouragement about our beloveds? Think about your personal relationship. Do you expend your time and energy replaying old records of how your partner drives you crazy with their bad habits? Remember, the more you focus on this, the more energy is created for the bad habits to remain, or worsen. Experiment with writing down all the positive attributes your beloved possesses. Focus on these traits. Compliment your partner on their humor or their willingness to help the underdog. Tell your love every day how much you adore and appreciate them. I promise you these endearments will never get old.

The fires from the twin flame union burn so brightly, others take notice. When the twins are together, other people feel the intensity of the connection, even if the two have not yet officially joined forces. The day after I met Daniel, I called my friend and psychic medium colleague Sally Rice. Sally got quite emotional as she said to me, "You just met your twin flame." Sally felt the force of the bond early on and emailed me a song she wanted to dedicate to our love. The song is titled "A Thousand Years," by singer and songwriter Christina Perri. The lyrics to this song are deep and profound. Shay Parker and her sister Angel gifted Daniel and me with a gorgeous picture frame for a wedding present with the words A Thousand Years written on it. This was truly a thoughtful gift that Daniel and I adore.

There were not any dry eyes on our wedding day, including mine and Daniel's. Grown men had tears streaming down their faces. The people who stood witness to our vows could feel the high vibration of our combined love. Daniel and I feel so blessed that all four of our parents were present for our forever promises to each other. My beautiful mom made her transition to the Spirit World only four short months later. I know beyond a shadow of a doubt that Mom made sure she didn't leave before beholding our sacred union. My mom also gifted Daniel and me with a song shortly after she met him. The song is called "Beautiful Mess," by Diamond Rio. Mom knew how special our relationship was and it brought her tremendous joy that Daniel had made his way into my life. I dedicate an entire chapter to my mom later in the book, as she was one of my soul mates in this lifetime.

Daniel is the love of my life. Instead of ever trying to hold me back as others have tried to do, he holds me up high and helps me put on my Angel Wings. When I have doubts, he reminds me of how strong I am. When others have hurt me through envy or jealousy, he encourages me to hold my head high and continue along the path of my life purpose. Daniel is my best friend. He dedicated a song to our love called "Into the Mystic" by Van Morrison. There is a verse that says,

I wanna rock your gypsy soul
Just like way back in the days of old
Then magnificently we will float
Into the mystic

The choice of this poetic song is so right because I AM a gypsy soul. Part of my soul contract is to live in various places, helping to "birth" an awakening or expansion in that area and then move on to the next place. It is no surprise that Daniel's soul contract also has the energy of traveler and rambler in it.

Have I mentioned yet that Daniel is also a medium? Shortly after we met, Daniel started telling me about experiences he had as a child and how he has seen the Spirit World. He shared a story with me about an experience he had at around the age of five. He and his grandfather were getting an ice cream cone. Daniel looked over and saw a flyer about a little girl who was missing in their area. On the ride home, Daniel told his grandfather that he knew where the little girl would be found. He pointed to an area as they drove by it. Sadly, the little girl's body was found a few days later in the exact location Daniel had told his grandfather about.

When Daniel's sister moved into her house, Daniel could see a teenage boy hanging out. Nobody else in the family could see this Spirit.

It's so interesting how many of us have seen, felt, or heard the Spirit World most of our lives, yet it feels uncomfortable to make the claim that we are mediums. Daniel has taken all levels of Psychic and Mediumship Development as well as attaining his Reiki Master certificate and yoga teacher certification and is embracing stepping forward to use his gifts to help others.

Daniel can see the Spirit World with his physical eyes. When he has attended some of my Mediumship Gallery Events where I bring forth messages from loved ones for certain people in the audience, Daniel has watched some of the loved ones file in for the occasion! He witnessed a husband standing proudly beside his wife, waiting his turn to connect. He observed a young boy walk into the room and sit next to his mom and grandmother and as I connected with him and brought through his messages of love, Daniel watched this boy smile a big smile of joy.

There have been a few times where I forgot to cut the cords from my reading. A psychic or medium must cut the energetic cords after each session as it's important we don't keep the energy of the reading in our field. Since Daniel can see the Spirit World with his physical eyes, he will lovingly point out that I must have forgotten to cut the cords. Daniel has said, "Honey, you brought a man home with you and he's standing by our bedroom door. Please cut the cords." At that point, I will look up and connect with the loved one and ask him or her to please respect my boundaries and my home life. Most of the time, they will comply with my request.

I chuckle as I think back to one night in our downtown loft in beautiful Asheville, NC. I was rudely awakened to a very large, menacing-looking man, standing at the foot of our bed. My scream woke Daniel up. I thought to myself, *Thank goodness I have my big strong protector here to save me from this intruder who is nosing around our bedroom from the Other World.* Seeing the threatening man, my big strong protector's automatic response was to push me in front of him, trying to hide behind me! Finally, as the spirit faded from our room, I exclaimed to Daniel, "Hey, I know we are both mediums, but you are the man medium, and you are supposed to protect me!" Daniel apologized for this little slip and we both got a good laugh out of it once our heartrates returned to their normal rhythms.

I wake up every day in tremendous gratitude that I have been blessed to share this lifetime with my twin flame. Even when the routines of life start to weigh me down, I take a deep breath and say a silent prayer of appreciation for the man who walks beside me.

Daniel, I have loved you for a thousand years and I will love you for who knows how many thousand more. Thank you for having the courage not to run during the times when the intensity of our union has ignited an inferno. Thank you for holding my mirror steady, enabling me to be the best version of myself possible. And above all else, thank you for holding me tight in the rare moments when the gravity of my mission overcomes me and the loneliness of being so different shakes me to the core of my soul. In your arms, I have found my true north.

Chapter 7

Losing Mom

As I sit down to write this chapter it is Mother's Day. I knew this would be the toughest chapter for me to write so I kept putting it off. And then, while everyone is out celebrating their moms on Mother's Day, I find myself in my writing room, ready to work on my book. I pondered, should I write Mom's chapter on Mother's Day? Will it make me even sadder than I already am today? As I tried to talk myself out of writing this chapter today, I felt Mom. I saw the sequence of 44 numbers, which is one way she sends me signs. I heard her say to me, *What better day to write this chapter than today?*

Before I talk about losing my mom, I want to tell you about who my mom is. My mom was not only my mom, she was my best friend and mentor. And my mom was a medium. So many of my friends and colleagues did not have support from their parents when it came to their gifts and being different. I have always felt very blessed in this way. My mom embraced my eccentric nature. I was never made to feel strange or bad about who I am.

I still laugh when I recall one memory of my mom. I was living with her at the time and we were sitting in the living room one morning, enjoying our coffee together. Mom asked me how I had slept the previous night. I then went on to explain that during the night I had been woken up by a Galactic Being who called himself Ashtar, of Ashtar Command, and that he told me he wished to work with my energy through my channeling. Mom didn't skip a beat as, lovingly chuckling, she said, "I'm so happy I have such a bizarre daughter who entertains me with her experiences! I wonder how many other moms have just had a conversation with their daughter over coffee about alien visitations?!"

I could talk to my mom about anything. Anything. There was no subject matter off limits. And Mom would call me out on my bullshit! Looking back, I am so happy she was not one of those moms who always takes your side whether you're in the right or wrong. She always, always had my back. Yet, she would lovingly point out ways that I could have handled things differently. And I grew stronger from that. For the mothers reading this book, whether your children are young or grown, I encourage you to take the same direction for your kids that my mom did for me. When they are in the right and someone is hurting them, stand proud and defend your babies as fiercely as a momma bear. But, when they are behaving badly themselves or treating someone in a way that is not honoring, gently call them out on it. No one is ever served by someone they love always telling them what they think they want to hear! Sometimes tough love is good love. It makes us stronger. It makes us want to be better.

My mom taught me that women can accomplish anything that men can! Though she was extremely smart, Mom was being held back in her career at the time in Jackson, Mississippi. She was a secretary for an insurance agency, and she wanted to keep moving up within the company. That was never going to happen at that time in Mississippi. So, Mom waited for me to graduate from high school and then moved to New Orleans. She knew New Orleans was more progressive and would offer her more opportunity to grow within her career. Her courage paid off. Over the years, Mom continued to move up, eventually becoming a vice president in her field! Watching her stand tall and proud, demanding to be treated equally and fairly, taught me much about the kind of person I would be.

My mom did not want to "claim" her gift of mediumship. She did not want the responsibility of it. It was a joke between us when she would say, "J, you are the medium. I'm not a medium." I would laugh and tell her, "Mom, you see and talk to dead people – that is the very definition of being a medium!" The experiences Mom had with the Spirit World were vast and astounding. She would have visits at night from beings she called "The Cloud People." She would tell us that when they visited, the entire room would fill up with these beings. It was always nighttime, yet she was wide awake. She could see the faces in the "clouds" in her room. Their presence always felt so loving that even though she was startled and caught off guard when they first appeared, she began to welcome her experiences with these beings.

My mom could hear music playing when there was no music in the room. Most of the time, it was music from the early 1900s. She enjoyed listening to these etheric tunes!

On one occasion many years ago, Mom was sad due to a breakup. She was standing in an aisle at a store, caught up in her thoughts. Out of nowhere, an African American man walked up to her and said in the most loving voice, "You are strong, and you are protected, and what you are going through right now shall pass." Mom recalled that he was radiant, and that his smile literally did light up the room. She felt safe, and the sadness lifted a bit. A second later she turned to thank him for his words, and he was gone. She ran up and down the aisles looking for this kind man, and he was not in the store. Mom knew she had been visited by an angel.

One time, I stayed with Mom for a few months shortly before I met Daniel. We were in her room one night, talking, when I shared, "Mom, there is a man sitting in your green chair. His cigarette smoke is overwhelming me, and he is giving me a dirty look!" Mom casually replied, "Yes, I know. He used to live here, and he enjoys visiting. He's harmless." This response is from the woman who claims she is *not* a medium!

The gift of my faith I owe to my mom. She did raise us as Southern Baptist, yet she grew away from religious doctrine over the years. She had a deep faith in God, yet it was the morals she taught my sister and me through her actions that reaped the greatest rewards. One particularly impressive example comes to mind that shows the type of person and woman my mom was. I was about 12 years old when Mom's best friend hurt her to her very core. Needless to say, my sister and I were angry at the woman. We knew her as she and her husband were friends with our parents. I know that if anything like this had happened to me as an adult, my angel wings would surely have retracted, and human Jill would have unleashed some fury! But not my mom. One night, she had my sister and me sit on her bed with her and hold hands in a circle. Mom said to us, "I got a message that we need to pray for Peggy." As an innocent young girl, I thought, *That is the last thing I want to do! Why would I pray for the woman who hurt my mom?* But as the three of us sat in a circle on Mom's bed that night, Mom prayed for the friend who had betrayed her. She prayed for the strength that would get us through this challenging time. This is the woman I had the privilege of calling Mom. She was also extraordinarily brave and strong. Shortly after she had moved in with me in Asheville, NC, she went for a routine female exam. The doctor called her the next day and told her she had ovarian cancer. We were in total shock. Looking back, I wish I had taken the time to properly tune in psychically or have a colleague tune in, but it all happened so quickly, and I had succumbed to fear over the possibility of losing my mom. Psychics and mediums do not operate or receive proper messages when they are engrossed in the lower vibrational energy of fear.

They scheduled Mom for surgery. When they opened her up, they found it was actually kidney cancer, not ovarian cancer. We later found out the doctor never even ordered the CA-125 blood test which would have shown she did not have ovarian cancer. When they opened her up, they exposed the cancer, so what would have been a stage 1 or stage 2 kidney cancer became a stage 4 kidney cancer, due to the doctor's error. That surgery gave the cancer oxygen to then travel to other parts of the body and into the bloodstream.

While Mom was in the hospital recovering from the surgery, my friend and colleague Leanna Marino called me and told me my mom's soul had come to her and had a conversation with her. Mom was in a hospital bed, resting. Leanna, who was in California, explained to me that Mom's lungs were filling up with fluid and she would die if something was not done immediately. I ran to get the nurse on duty. I asked her to check Mom's lungs. She blew me off and said everything was just fine. I could not get anyone to pay attention to me. I went back to the room and told my sister Wendy that I was probably going to be arrested because I was about to cause a scene like they had never witnessed before. I told her to stay with Mom and take care of her. It was later in the evening. I walked down to the nurse's station and saw all the nurses gathered together, gabbing as if they were at a party. I very politely asked again for them to page my mom's doctor. They declined. I began yelling at the top of my lungs, demanding that someone get Mom's doctor. Instead of the doctor, they called security. Security showed up right away. The officer told me to get my shoes on so he could escort me from the building. I looked this man in his eyes and asked him, "If you knew your mama was in danger and nobody would help her, would you do what I'm doing?" I added, "I am a psychic medium, and a colleague has connected with my mom who tells her she needs her doctor ASAP, or she will die." The security guard, responded, "If it were my mama, I would be doing the same thing you are right now." He went on, "Instead of me escorting you from the building, I will be ordering them to call the doctor." With a sweet smile he assured me, "Your mama is lucky to have you." No sir, I am the lucky one.

The doctor on call was not happy with me. As he entered the room, he argued with me, insisting that my mom's lungs were crystal clear. I explained that he was wrong. I told him of Leanna's message to me about Mom's lungs filling up with fluid. I demanded he order an X-ray. You could see the sinister glint in his eyes as I read his thoughts: *You want me to order an X-ray because some loony psychic in California spoke to your mom, who is lying here in this bed thousands of miles away from her in North Carolina, just because the psychic says her lungs are filling up with fluid. Yeah, right!* They knew enough about me by that point not to argue with me any further. He ordered the X-ray. When it showed Mom's lungs indeed filling with fluid, they sprang into action, ordering an immediate procedure to drain the fluid. Mom would have died then, had it not been for Leanna. None of the doctors or nurses ever apologized to me about what happened. But my mom survived that experience. I will always owe great gratitude to Leanna for saving Mom that night.

The next few weeks were spent recovering and finding a kidney specialist. After consulting with the specialist, it was determined that the tumors on her kidneys were vast. The next step in her journey was to have an entire kidney removed, as well as half of the other one. The chance of Mom not being on dialysis afterwards was slim to none. I can't tell you how strong my mom was during those months.

The pain was excruciating. She was very weak. But she stayed strong and persevered through both surgeries. The next hurdle came quickly.

I accompanied Mom to the oncologist. The oncologist looked at Mom's reports and then looked up at her and said, "Go home and get your affairs in order. Say goodbye to your loved ones. You have only three months to live." Mom and I were in shock. We both started bawling. I then gathered my composure enough to ask the doctor about whether changing the diet would help. I had changed my diet to vegan years prior and reversed my illnesses. I had watched many documentaries where people had reversed cancer, type II diabetes, autoimmune diseases, high blood pressure, high cholesterol, and many other ailments simply by eating a plant-based diet. The doctor looked at my mom and said, "Diet will not help you. Go eat anything you want and enjoy it."

We got out to the car and I looked over at my beautiful mother as she was sobbing. I said, "Mom, do you want to live? Are you ready to continue this fight?" She said, yes, without a doubt. I then explained that she would need to start eating only plant-based food right away. She responded that she had eaten meat her entire life and didn't know if she could give it up. I repeated, "If you want to save your life, you will do it."

Mom embraced plant-based living with full tenacity. I was so very proud of her! Her doctors were in complete shock. Due to her healthy eating, her kidney levels were normal, and no dialysis was ever needed. The doctors had never seen a patient with only half a kidney maintaining perfect blood levels. The three-month prognosis came and went. Every time she went in for a checkup and scan, the report came back cancer free. They called Mom a miracle woman.

I invite each of you to begin shifting your viewpoint of doctors. Doctors are not God. They are humans, and most of them have been through a training sponsored primarily by the pharmaceutical companies. Most medical schools teach fewer than 25 hours of nutrition! After all those years in medical school, most doctors have the same solution, patient after patient. Write another script for yet another pharmaceutical, and/or perform surgery, even if only exploratory. God blessed us with herbs and flowers and plants that provide all the healing our bodies need! Pharmaceutical companies can't patent nature or herbs, so they add harmful chemicals to the herbs in order to patent and profit from it. I am not expressing that doctors are not needed. Surgeons are needed. I am simply offering a thought-provoking way to take charge of your own life, health, and well-being. Learn to question everything a doctor tells you. If it doesn't feel right, don't do it. If a doctor writes you a script, consider consulting with a naturopath or herbalist to see if there is a natural alternative that has a similar or even greater success rate. Much information is also available for you to sift through online. A beautiful feeling of empowerment comes from taking charge of our personal healing journey. If you haven't done so already, I encourage you to start learning about proper nutrition and what foods best serve our physical bodies.

Hippocrates said it best: "Let food be thy medicine, and medicine be thy food." Many times, we pay more attention to the fuel we put into our cars than the fuel we put into our bodies. As you can see, I am a huge proponent of plant-based eating. It has changed my life. And it saved my mom's life for many years until another doctor ended up lying to her.

Three years went by with no cancer. When a small cancerous growth came back, we decided to take Mom to a 30-day natural healing hospital in Mexico, because many of their life-saving protocols are illegal in the United States. I stayed with her the first two weeks and my sister was with her for the last two. I can't sing enough praises about the doctors and their staff! Compassion was overflowing, and the level of care was second to none. The doctor explained to Mom that it would take time for the small tumor to disappear and for her not to fear it. With natural healing, we must give our bodies time to return to perfect and divine order. Our bodies are powerful beyond measure!

Everything was moving along beautifully. Mom was doing really well, and our family bonds had grown even stronger based on everything we had been through over the past few years. This is the part of the story that is different because I am a medium. I knew when my mom was going to die. I didn't want to know this. I didn't ask for the information. My grandmother in Spirit just thought that I needed to know. I was in yoga class one January day, trying to enjoy my Shavasana after an exhilarating yoga practice. For those of you who have not yet tried yoga, shavasana is the pose at the end of practice where you get to lie on your mat in total relaxation. It's yummy, and always so treasured when it comes time for this pose. As I was trying to enjoy my shavasana, my grandmother came in and said to me, "Your mom will be leaving you soon. You need to prepare yourself. She will be making her transition in September." I was in shock. I ran from the room, tears flowing. I called Wendy. I always first ask her if she wants to know what I've been told. She said she did want to know. I was sobbing as I relayed the message from Gran. Wendy suggested that maybe Gran was wrong. I can assure you -- this would have been one of the times I would pray to be wrong. My beautiful mother passed away on August 28th, three days before the fated September prediction.

As mediums, we are given information that frankly sometimes we just don't want to know. I'm sure my grandmother knew best in that it gave me time to *sort of* prepare myself. Yet, death is something you can never really prepare yourself for.

Psychics and mediums can also see things play out in ways they may not want to see or know. The visions just come in. When my mother called me in February saying she had decided to have radiation, I was shown a vision of her dying from the effects of the radiation. The vision was as clear as if I were watching TV. I started crying and begged her not to have the radiation. I screamed, I "If you have the radiation, you will die!" Mom was quite upset and told me that what I said wasn't very nice. She felt I was not being supportive of her decision. After I calmed down from what my vision had shown me, my grandmother's message from the month prior came rushing back in. I could not tell my mom of her mother's visit to me and the message she gave. After all, my mother was fighting for her life. This was one of the most challenging times of my life. Thank God my husband Daniel was there to help me through this. I was so angry at Mom for not paying attention to my prophecy and my knowing. She knew my accuracy was quite high. She knew that when the oncologist had given her three months, my protocol of plant-based eating, natural herbs, and Reiki saved her life. Yet, she was hell-bent on listening to this doctor. I told her he was lying to her. I told her she did not need radiation. My mom began her radiation in March and was dead by August. By the way, my prediction was validated and proven a few months before she passed away, but it was too late. A spinal specialist told Mom that she had **not** needed the radiation, and that its effects had irreversibly worsened her situation. The radiation had caused the small tumor to grow and press against the nerves of her spine. My sister and I still suffer PTSD from listening to Mom's animalistic screams from her pain; there was no relief for her because she was allergic to morphine and they could not get the pain under control. Emotionally, I was at the lowest point I've ever been. Why had she chosen not to listen to me, when she knew how strong my gifts are? I was angry at her for leaving us. I was furious that although she had fought so hard against all the odds and won, she still chose to listen to some random doctor who sealed her fate for her.

One thing this nightmare taught me is that we must honor and allow our loved ones to chart their own course. Can you imagine how difficult this is for us as mediums or psychics who often know what will happen if our loved one doesn't listen to us? It's unbearable. Throughout those months between January and August, I vacillated between anger and deep grief. My mother knew how accurate my predictions were. Yet, she chose to listen to some asshole radiologist who just wanted the money from her unnecessary treatments. It took me a very long time to release these strong emotions. Just writing about it brings back all the pain and helplessness.

Now that I have had time to process and reflect, I must admit that there is a possibility my mom left simply because it was her time to leave. Maybe her karma was complete for this lifetime. A few mediums have given me that message from my mom. She had special work to do on the Other Side. Several mediums have channeled messages from Mom about the work she is doing with the trees and nature. A wonderful channel named Lucy Finch called me shortly after my mother's transition, telling me that Mom had visited her. Lucy explained that Mom was on the Other Side, helping to heal the planet by working with its vegetation. Mom loved gardening. She would create the most beautiful oases in her yards. So it makes perfect sense that Mom is working with Gaia, helping our natural world. This beautiful message from Lucy brought me so much comfort during my intense grief.

I'm not sure about other mediums, but I know for myself that this has been one of the greatest challenges to overcome: knowing outcomes and seeing visions, yet understanding that it is not our job to control or orchestrate anyone's journey.

We don't always know the entire story of the karma or the soul's longing. If someone gives us permission, we can share the knowing or vision with them. Yet, what they choose to do with that information is determined by their own free will.

Many of you have heard the term "the new normal." When we lose a loved one who was very close to us, our lives are never the same. We are different people in what seems to be a whole different world. The grief can even affect us physically.

If I were made to find a silver lining from losing my mom, it would be this: I am a better medium. I am a better medium because I have pure unadulterated empathy when I am telling a client how sorry I am for their loss. Before losing my mom, I thought I could imagine the gut-wrenching grief many of my clients were going through. Frankly, I had no clue. You don't know what you don't know. Now, when I tell them how sorry I am for the loss of their loved one, the compassion and empathy in my words are wholly informed and completely sincere. The truth is realized from having experienced the same situation yourself.

I am also a better medium because my mom had the same gift, and I know she helps me from the Other Side. And my beautiful mom is still keeping me in line! I recall a day recently when my nerves had kicked in because I had a public mediumship gallery later that night. Every medium I know still gets nervous and feels butterflies before they go on stage in front of an audience. It's just part of being human. I was having a salt cave session to calm my nerves and clear my energy field when Mom came to me very strongly. As always, as soon as I felt her, I started to cry. She loved on me and then affectionately told me to let go of my nerves. She said, "This is not about you. This is about people showing up, hoping to hear messages from their loved ones and get validation that they have survived their physical bodies. When your nerves kick in, immediately change your line of thinking and consider how *you* would be feeling if *you* were going to a gallery hoping to hear from me." She reminded me that I am simply the conduit and channel, and as long as I remembered that, the Spirit World would never let me down. Hearing from her shifted everything for me! My nerves eased up a bit. We were pulling out of the parking lot and I was telling Daniel about the visitation from Mom. Amazingly, the car right in front of us had the license plate 3Graces. This is what my mom, sister, and I called ourselves -- The 3Graces! My sister even put together a beautiful framed puzzle for me titled 3Graces. I have never in my life seen a license plate that read 3Graces! Yet, there it was, right in front of me. I cried as I thanked Mom for the additional sign from heaven that she was always with me and supporting me in my work.

After Mom's passing, an interesting thing happened with my sister, Wendy, who is not a medium. She began to receive visits from Mom in which Mom would rub her leg or run her fingers through Wendy's hair. There were times when Wendy's signs and experiences were much stronger than my own! Wendy and I consider ourselves very lucky to have had each other after Mom's death. Even though we grieved separately and in our own way, we are always there for each other when we need to process our emotions or discuss how much it hurts to have this void in our lives. It has always frustrated me when someone has made the comment, "Your sister isn't gifted. She is not a medium." Wendy may not have chosen to be a medium in this lifetime, but she is far from being without gifts! Wendy's gifts are vast. She is one of the best mothers I have ever known. She is creative in ways beyond imagining and is extremely smart. Wendy has run a very successful company, and has long had the ability to transform a room into something that deserves to be featured in a magazine. I have always adored her hilarious humor. She is one of those people who can make you laugh without trying! Wendy accepts me for who I am and loves me no matter how strange I can be at times. I thank God every day for my beautiful sister.

Even though Wendy chose not to come in with the mediumship gift this lifetime, her children do have the gift.

Both her daughters could see and communicate with spirits as children. Her son Tyler, who is now only 13 years old, is a medium. Mom has come to Tyler to let him know she is always around. And there is a woman in spirit he can hear singing from time to time. Tyler has expressed interest in my psychic and mediumship classes when he gets a little older. I look forward to helping him follow his path!

I can't tell you how many people have said to me, "Well, losing your mom must be much easier since you are a medium. At least you can communicate with her all the time." This assumption could not be further from the truth! Being a medium does not make losing my mom one bit easier. Just because I know she is in a better place and free of her pain does not mean that I don't grieve not having her here with me in the physical. I miss her terribly, every day. There is not a day that goes by that I don't feel the loss. Those of you who have lost loved ones know what I am talking about. As Tracy Lawrence sings, time marches on. We simply learn to awaken to each new day with courage and grace. Some days are easier than others.

In closing this chapter, I'd like to pause to send each of you a big virtual healing hug if you have lost someone in your life who meant as much to you as my mom means to me. With this virtual hug comes some important guidance. Do your best not to stop living life because of your grief. Give yourself time and permission to grieve. However, don't let anyone tell you how long that grieving should be, or what it should look like. It's different for everyone. The best gift you can give your loved ones in heaven is this: Fully discover your life purpose and embrace it to the best of your ability. Have faith. Be brave. As you welcome the dawn of each new day, stand tall and speak your truth. Courageously step forward being the best version of the person you came here to be.

I love you more, Momma.

Chapter 8
Passion, Purpose, & Sacred Travel

One thing I have realized as I travel my own personal path is that our path is rarely laid out in a straight line for us. What I have discovered for myself, as well as my clients and students, is that many times our path is a winding and somewhat bumpy one, with quite a few roadblocks along the way. The key is to learn to welcome and even embrace the detours. After all, our spirit guides have our backs. They know what we chose for our soul growth opportunities. They can see the soul contracts that we agreed to prior to being born into this lifetime.

Until we understand what our soul purpose is, we may feel as if our path has been washed away in a monsoon. And when life brings us challenge after challenge, we may indeed feel as if we are bracing ourselves each day to move through a veritable storm. You have probably heard the adage, "God does not give you more than you can handle." It is my belief that God gave us free will. Therefore, it's not up to God to determine what our challenges are. We chose our soul growth opportunities ourselves with the assistance of our spirit guides before we incarnated. This is another reason why a good intuitive development course is so beneficial. During the course, you should be given the opportunity to establish a relationship with your spirit guides. You learn how to tune in to your aura and energy, and how to work within the frameworks of your own individual gifts. As you explore and discover more about your soul's essence, the fog begins to lift, and the portal that opens to your path seems brighter, more enticing, and easier to follow.

It felt imperative that I include this chapter for several reasons. About 75% of the thousands of clients I have had over the years have no conscious awareness of their soul's purpose. This is one reason I am so passionate about sharing my knowledge, experience, and wisdom as a spiritual teacher. Learning to tap into your intuition is one spoke in the wheel towards discovering your contracts and purpose. What I have discovered for myself over the years by studying with my amazing spiritual teachers is that many times throughout our lives, new contracts present themselves to us. The key is to determine whether something new is indeed one of your soul contracts or a distraction. And yes, sometimes distractions are put in place to help us further clarify and learn to listen to our soul's guidance.

As you proceed along the path to discovering who you are on a soul level, be aware of the physical changes that start to occur as you raise your vibrations. You may have heard this referred to as ascension symptoms. I can assert to you that this is very real. As we welcome new energy into our physical bodies, it can sometimes feel uncomfortable, as higher frequencies vibrate faster. When we agree to clear out old thought patterns and beliefs, it may even feel like our lives have been turned upside down. And many times, they are. Some of my clients and students have reported that all hell broke loose in their lives as they begin to step into the reality of who they really are. It is Spiritual Law that certain vibrations can't coexist in the same frequency of different vibrations. Therefore, it makes perfect sense why certain friends, loved ones, and family members may start feeling uncomfortable in your presence as you allow new energy to come in. They may feel like they don't know who you are any longer. This is part of the process of letting go of your ego self as you strive to welcome more of the Christ Consciousness into your physical mind and body.

Some of the physical symptoms you may experience as you begin to awaken and increase your vibration are headaches, nausea, vertigo, ringing in the ears, or shooting pains throughout the body. For me personally, my teeth and jaw would also hurt and feel weird. At times, you may experience a bizarre pulsating feeling reverberating throughout your body. When you are allowing more of your

Light Body to come in, you will need more rest. I have spoken to many people who claimed they needed to rest so often that they began to feel a bit lazy. If this is happening to you, allow your body this time of rest! I'm not suggesting that you sit around all day, eating bonbons, while claiming to everyone that you are ascending! But it does mean that we must tune in to what our bodies need at various times in our journey of awakening.

Nor am I suggesting that everyone who has headaches, nausea, or ringing in the ears is going through their ascension process. It goes without saying that a doctor's visit is vital to rule out medical causes for these physical ailments. But, when a doctor can find no rational explanation for your complaints, you may indeed be going through what we refer to as upgrades to your physical body to bring in more of your Light Body.

Many people report changes in their eating habits, showing up as cravings or aversions to certain foods. Things they would previously eat start turning their stomachs. Others report changes in their sensitivity to smells and odors.

The good news is that these symptoms come in waves or shifts. You will not feel these uncomfortable sensations constantly. Meditation, Reiki, and yoga can help to relieve some of the physical as well as the emotional symptoms associated with your awakening process.

The silver lining to these changes is that positive things happen through the ascension process. You experience bliss more often. You learn to be in the present moment and truly appreciate nature. How many of us go through our day without once acknowledging the remarkable gifts we are given from nature's bounty? I encourage you to start thanking the trees for all they so lovingly bestow. Take time from your day to tune in to the songs of the birds. I have recently channeled the information that birds come from a higher dimension, and their songs are offered not only to delight, but also to heal us. How cool is that?

As you awaken, you will start experiencing an increase in synchronicities and signs. There is a joke among the spiritual community that some people claim everything is a sign. Folks, sometimes it's just a normal occurrence! Everything that happens is not a sign from the Universe! But many, many things are.

As you begin to release old patterns of belief and conditioning and start allowing more of your Light Body to express, it becomes much easier to tune into what you came here to accomplish. As they awaken, some people report feeling a "knowing" that they have a divine purpose on the planet, or that they are here on a special mission. I can promise you that every one of us is! We each have a soul purpose, or several, and have agreed to events and experiences that offer opportunities for our souls to grow.

There are entire books written about the ascension or awakening process. If you have never heard of this, I encourage you to research and learn more about it. It helps to know we are not alone in what we are experiencing and feeling.

Spiritual Teaching

I have learned so much from my spiritual teachers and mentors. I have heard some mediums say, "I was born with the gift; hence, I don't need a spiritual teacher." Wake up, y'all! This is pure ego! Can you imagine if Tiger Woods claimed that he is the greatest golfer of all time, and therefore had no further need to practice? This is nonsense. We all learn from one another every day. I would like to give a shout out to the spiritual teachers I have studied with over the years, as each one of them helped to refine who I am as a person and a medium. Alfred Ricci, Hans Christian King, John Holland, Janet Nohavec, Lisa Williams, Mavis Pittilla, Colin Bates, Sharon Klingler, and several remarkable mediums at Arthur Findlay College, in England. Arthur Findlay is the world's foremost college for the advancement of spiritualism and psychic sciences. I learned something valuable from each of these teachers.

One of my greatest accolades as a medium came when I found out that Hans Christian King, prior to his passing, had chosen me as one of the two mediums he would entrust his clients of over 60 years to. I was in awe simply to be in this profound medium's presence, as his connection to the World of Spirit was pure and sublime. I highly recommend Hans's book, *Guided Reclaiming the Intuitive Voice of Your Soul*. The words of wisdom from this great spiritual teacher and direct voice medium flow effortlessly through you from the pages of this book.

It would take many years before I listened to the calling to answer and agree to one of my personal soul contracts. As I previously admitted, my spirit guide, Saisha, says I can be quite stubborn at times! I did agree on a soul level to offer spiritual teachings to many people. However, I was at first reluctant to step up to the plate and declare myself a teacher. One of my pet peeves over the years that I have been teaching is when a student takes one class and then declares that they are now a spiritual teacher. For mediumship teaching, the instructor must be able to establish a connection with the same Spirit Communicator that his or her student is communicating with. This takes years and years of practice to master.

My first nudging from my Spirit Team came when my clients began asking me to teach them psychic development. I resisted and resisted. Then, at a Best American Psychics spiritual retreat, one of my colleagues, Marc Lainhart, came up to me and said he was guided to give me a gift. The gift was a beautiful polished stone with the word "teacher" on it. OK, Spirit, I'm going to listen now! I still have this thoughtful gift from Marc on my altar. This is a perfect example of how messages from our spirit guides, angels, and loved ones can come in packages you could never dream possible. Learn to pay attention to your own messages. Be open to the extraordinary ways Spirit will attempt to get your attention.

One thing I have discovered throughout the years I have been teaching is that each class is not simply comprised of one teacher and many students. My students have shared with me how much they have learned from me and what a great teacher I am. At the same time, I have personally learned much from my students as well. This is one of the advantages of participating in an in-person class. Class discussions and the questions asked by fellow students provide a perfect setting for further exploration and expansion of the topic at hand. My pride runs deep with the Mississippi Academy for Spiritual Development I have created within our Spiritual Center. People are traveling from all over the country to participate in our programs.

Psychic Investigations

Another soul contract that presented itself along the way has to do with psychic investigations. Again, this is not something I sought. Time and time again I was asked to help with a missing persons or unsolved case, either by the loved one's family or someone in the Spirit World. To my dismay, I found that quite a few law enforcement officers and private investigators are not at all open to working with a psychic detective. This is so careless. Psychics and mediums are not attempting to take the place of the usual investigators, or to disturb protocol. We are simply given information from the Spirit World that offers clues that may help solve a case.

I have found that psychic detective work has better results when more than one psychic is tuning in. This is why we have formed groups of professional psychics and mediums to look to the Spirit World for clues, hints, and answers.

In my personal experience, various members of the group of psychics will receive different clues. When we put them all together, it's like putting a puzzle together with all the missing pieces. For instance, in one case we were trying to locate a body. The police were not even searching for it as they considered this a missing person's case, even though the person had been missing for 14 months. One psychic received the name of an overlook point by a river. Most of us saw the body close to a river. One psychic saw railroad tracks. Another was shown shipping containers and an industrial type building with loading docks and trucks. I was shown an old white building that was some kind of convenience store. I also kept hearing the name "Hideaway." Once I'd put all these clues together, I decided to drive around in the area of the river. I came across a lookout with the exact name one of my colleagues had been given. I started getting goose bump chills, which means I am getting close to finding what I am searching for. A few yards down the street, I came across the old white convenience store the man in spirit had shown me. Directly behind this store were the railroad tracks. Next to the store was the building with the loading docks and trucks, and on the railroad track behind all of this were the shipping containers! And for the cherry on top, the name Hideaway that I had been given ended up being a bar down the street from where I was! When you have a detective or private investigator open to receiving such clues, many more cases are solved.

This work is not for every psychic or medium. Many times, our insights are depressing and filled with trauma and grief. The things we "witness" in our visions are often quite disturbing. Those of us who are called to help with this type of psychic work have learned to put up a sort of wall or barrier to protect ourselves from feeling too much of the trauma.

In one case I was asked to work on, I knew the college girl who was missing was still alive. I was shown that she was being held in a very remote area. Unfortunately, her family and the private investigator were not open to working with a psychic detective. The PI was in fact quite rude when I called him, offering to help. The irony was that I was offering my services pro bono! What did they have to lose? I told him she was still alive. I gave some names and directions I had been given. The PI admitted that a few other psychics had called him with similar information. Yet, they did nothing with it. I recall the day I knew the missing girl had joined the Spirit World. My heart was broken. I felt that I should have done more. Maybe I should have flown to the area and tried to locate her myself, without the assistance of the PI. I had to let it go and come to terms with the fact that it was not my responsibility and that I had done the best I could to help.

So yes -- this work can be emotionally draining and disturbing. It is certainly a calling. Frustrations run high when law enforcement refuses to acknowledge any of the clues or information received. This is especially so when the departed is continually begging for our assistance in helping to bring justice or offer closure to their family members. However, I am proud I answered the calling to help in whatever ways I can.

<u>Sacred Travel</u>

Another soul contract presented to me later in life regards sacred travel to areas of the world that are comprised of special energy. Our Mother Earth is a living being, infused with invisible subtleties, such as chakras, meridians, vortexes, portals, and pressure points.

Once you begin tuning in to your physical body, including the astral and auric energy fields, you will be able to pinpoint areas or places within planet Earth that resonate in an easy way or a more challenging way with your physical body. Even people who have never studied energy can feel the various energetic pulsations in these special places on the planet.

Earth's energy field can be detected by using dowsing rods, pendulums, or even a compass. Many believe ancient ley lines are entwined with sacred geometry, which resonates with me as well. This is a fascinating subject to explore!

What is the difference between Earth energy and ley lines? Earth energy encompasses all. Just as humans, plants, and animals are comprised of energy, so too is our entire planet. Some perceive the energy as positive or negative, depending on the location and how it responds to their personal chakras and meridians.

Ley lines are straight lines between two points which appear to align with geographical landmarks and structures of religious and spiritual significance. The concept was first introduced in the 1920s by businessman, photography pioneer, and amateur archaeologist Alfred Watkins, in England. Watkins studied and wrote about ancient sites and alignments of geographical and historical interest, natural and man-made. Books on ley lines, portals, vortexes, and earth chakras open a fascinating area that you might wish to explore.

The basic difference between a vortex and a portal is simple. Vortexes are energy spirals that can be scientifically measured in some places. Portals are doorways and openings to other dimensions. Although portals have not yet been scientifically accepted, some scientists are currently working to prove their existence, along with the reality of parallel universes. Another fascinating subject! As a professional psychic, I am able to tune in to portals and feel the energetic difference when I am standing in one. Oftentimes hauntings and other spirit activity are more active in a home or building that has had a portal open up. It acts as a sort of gateway for entry from other dimensions. As with human beings, entities entering through portals can be both positive and negative. If you feel you may have an open portal in your home and are experiencing hauntings or disturbing phenomena of any kind, consult with a professional shaman or medium who performs rituals to close the portal and clear the space.

One day, from out of the blue, my Spirit Team spoke to me, as they are occasionally wont to do. The message I was given was this: *It is now time for you to begin your sacred travel. You will accompany groups of people to sacred land consisting of revered ley lines and ancient energy. Over time, you will visit each of the chakras of Mother Earth. This process has multiple layers to it, as those who choose to accompany you must be willing to receive and release some of their own energy to the land. These sacred trips are not only about each person receiving the benefits of the sacred energy. They are for each person to also bring their individual energy to each place, and leave some of it behind to help heal Mother Earth.*

I was elated after hearing this message! What a cool assignment I had been given! So far, I have led groups to Mount Shasta, California, Sedona, Arizona, Glastonbury, England, and Stonehenge, in Wiltshire, England. Visiting and connecting to the energy of these ancient places, can truly assist us along our path of spiritual growth and expansion.

With the poles shifting slightly, the chakras of Mother Earth can also shift a bit and encompass larger areas. For instance, some consider Mount Shasta to be the root chakra of Mother Earth. Others believe that Sedona, Arizona, is the root chakra. The root chakra is all about grounding and connecting to the earth. The color associated with this chakra is red. It has a denser feeling than some of the higher chakras. After spending time in both Mount Shasta and Sedona, I personally feel root chakra energy in both places.

In August of 2017, Sally Rice and I led a group to Mount Shasta to experience the total solar eclipse. What a powerful place to be during such a momentous event. A truly magical experience! We would sit on the deck at night and watch the UFO activity, as it is quite prevalent in that area. When you hike in the mountains of Shasta, you can certainly feel the different vortexes and portals of energy.

Most people feel that Lake Titicaca and Machu Picchu, Peru, are connected to the second chakra of Mother Earth. This chakra is known as the sacral or creative chakra and helps us tune in to our creative expression as well as our sexuality. The color associated with the sacral chakra is orange. The element of this chakra is water, so it makes sense that Lake Titicaca is associated with this chakra. There are so many ways to express our creativity. Native lore has it that Lake Titicaca was created by the rainbow serpent and is where primal energy itself is born. Therefore, Lake Titicaca is an ideal place to connect to our kundalini energy. What exactly is kundalini? Kundalini refers to the vital force or life force energy that we all have within us. It is also sometimes called the "sleeping goddess" and is usually represented as a serpent coiled around the root chakra at the base of the spine. Some people have been known to experience sudden kundalini awakenings, but for most people, this is a gradual process.

We are planning our group travel to Lake Titicaca and Machu Picchu during the Leo New Moon in August of 2020. New moons are wonderful times to set new intentions and celebrate new beginnings. We will explore ways to work and expand our personal kundalini energy. We will perform sacred ceremony centering on clearing any old energy blockages along our spines so that the kundalini may continue to rise. Shamans will accompany us to help remove stagnant or misplaced energy in the physical body, the etheric aura, and the astral aura. I'm super excited that I'll be journeying to the sacral chakra of Mother Earth next year!

The third chakra, also known as the solar plexus chakra, is the link between the mind and the emotions. It is the chakra that connects us to our will and personal power. Yellow is the color associated with this chakra, and its element is fire. When we truly immerse ourselves in the energy of this chakra, it can help us with our self-confidence and even our identity. The area connected to Mother Earth's solar plexus chakra is Ayers Rock, Uluru, Australia. According to Aboriginal legend, this area is the "umbilical cord" of the planet, and is estimated to be around 600 million years old! When we travel here for our sacred journey, we will be working on clearing our ancestral wounds and removing old densities that may be trapped from previous lifetimes. This sacred land in Uluru has been known to empower seekers to remember who they are and what they came here to do. Of course, it makes sense that this Mama Gaia chakra resonates to the tones of this energy since our solar plexus chakra is all about our identity. What better location to help heal the planet than the place connected to the umbilical cord?

Glastonbury, England, is the heart chakra of Mother Earth. The fourth or heart chakra focuses on compassion and Universal Truth. The color associated with this chakra is green and the element is air. This chakra is said to be the bridge between the earthly plane and spiritual plane. The lower three chakras are more connected to the Earth plane, and the higher chakras are connected to the spiritual plane; therefore, the heart is the link between the two. This chakra helps us to love, forgive, and accept. As we ascend into higher dimensions, it is vital that we learn to love ourselves first, and above all others. Learning this can be challenging for some people, especially sensitives who are used to giving.

However, because this imperative is of critical importance, I urge you to begin working on loving yourself above all others right away. Start each day by looking in the mirror and exclaiming, "I love you!" What a beautiful way to begin each day.

Glastonbury is also the home of the Holy Grail. Author Dan Brown excited a great deal of interest in the Holy Grail in his best-selling books. According to The Legend of King Arthur and His Knights, the Holy Grail was an actual cup used by Christ at the Last Supper, and the Knights Templar were entrusted with the mission to protect it. Legend has it that Joseph transported the Holy Grail to Avalon, a legendary island which came to be identified with Glastonbury.

Some people maintain that the Holy Grail is a mystical code representing the bloodline of Jesus and Mary Magdalene. There are some early Christian texts that depict Mary Magdalene as not just a follower of Jesus, but his trusted companion. Some have interpreted these texts to mean that she was his wife. It is my personal belief that Jesus and Mary Magdalene were married and did have children. I have a huge affinity with Mary Magdalene and the M in my middle name is in honor of her. It angers me that churches and pastors have long portrayed her as a prostitute. This in my opinion is a clear example of those in power trying to downplay the importance of women and the roles women play. Why is it that Jesus cannot be both an extraordinary prophet and a man who dearly loves and cherishes his wife? I believe he was both, and that Mary of Magdala was his beloved.

When our group traveled to Glastonbury and visited the Tor, the Chalice Well, Avebury, and Stonehenge, it was truly life changing. Daniel and I have both had past lives in and around this area, so for us personally, it felt like coming home. My spirit guide Saisha shared lifetimes with me in England. When Daniel and I did ceremony at the Chalice Well, we both shed tears from the deep intensity of the emotions we had connected to this ancient place. If you ever have the chance to travel to this sacred land, I hope you will do so. Being in the physical presence of the monolithic stones of Avebury and Stonehenge is magical and mystical, to say the least. Our group received special permission to go inside the stone circles of Stonehenge, and we left behind certain crystals and stones forever connecting this magnificent energy with the energy where each of us resides.

The fifth chakra is known as the throat chakra, which governs self-expression and speaking our truth. The color associated with this chakra is a bright blue. The Great Pyramids near Mt. Sinai in Egypt are connected to Mother Earth's throat chakra. The Great Pyramid of Khufu (a.k.a. Giza) is thirty times more capacious in cubic volume than the

Empire State Building, though the latter is, of course, much taller. Its base covers 13 acres. This is the oldest structure in existence, over 4,600 years old, and is the sole survivor of the Seven Wonders of the World. The corners of the pyramid align with the cardinal points on a compass. Its northern shadow and southern reflection of sun precisely mark the dates of solstices and equinoxes. This is truly one of the most mysterious places on the planet.

The sixth chakra, better known as the third eye chakra, has to do with our intuitive selves. Its color is indigo or purple, and it is associated with the pineal gland. Clairvoyance, telepathy, and precognition are experienced through this chakra. The third eye is the center where we may transcend duality – the assumption of "I" as a discrete and separate entity, fundamentally apart from all else. Through it, portals open, connecting to extra-dimensional energy. Just as our pineal gland enables us to recognize other dimensions and realities, this chakra of Gaia has the same benefits. This is one Mother Earth chakra that appears to change location. It is believed to be in Western Europe, close to Glastonbury. In the next age, many feel this Mother Earth Chakra will relocate to Brazil.

The crown or seventh chakra is governed by the color violet/purple. This chakra is associated with balancing mind, body, and spirit. Precognition and claircognizance are awakened here. The Mother Earth chakra associated with the seventh chakra is in Mt. Kailas, Tibet. This is a very sacred mountain in the Himalayas, and many believe it to be the crown of creation or the roof of the world. The Tibetan people, as evidenced through the Dalai Lama's teachings, are known for their highly developed consciousness. It makes perfect sense that this would be the location of Gaia's crown chakra, as it connects us to all that is.

Of course, there are many other places that hold higher energy vortexes and portals. When we visit these sacred sites and energy vortexes and blend our personal energy fields with the energy of these places, our lives are forever changed. From each place I have visited, I bring back its unique frequency or energy signature. Friends and family can even notice the change in our energy fields when we return. If sacred travel is something that interests you, I invite you to sign up for my Newsletter so you will be notified of upcoming voyages and adventures.

In closing this chapter, I would like to reemphasize the importance of discovering your own passions. By tuning in to our passions, we are often led to pieces and fragments of our purpose. We don't incarnate with only one single soul purpose. We have chosen several, all of which can have varied effects and importance at different times in our lives.

In other words, our purpose can shapeshift over the course of our lives. Please don't ever feel that you are too old to step into one of your passions or purposes. This is simply not true. We are never too old to start over, change direction, or even blaze new trails.

In fact, as you gracefully age, I encourage you to practice becoming funkier, and more avant-garde. Strive to become a pioneer with your personal passions! Be that family member your relatives are still talking about years after your transition to the Other World! Make an impact in some way that brings deeper meaning to your life. I promise you will thank me for this advice one day!

Chapter 9

Full Circle Home

When I first brought my love Daniel to visit Mississippi, I asked him what his thoughts were as we were driving back to Asheville, North Carolina. His reply: "It's beautiful and I love your family, but don't ever ask me to move there." Daniel was a North Carolina boy, born and raised, and he began his awakening after his move to the mountains of Asheville. Back then, I had no plans of moving back to Mississippi, so all was well. After Daniel asked me to marry him and I responded with a resounding yes, I did disclose a key component of what it would mean being married to me. I explained that I always listened to the guidance and direction of my Spirit Team. I went on to clarify that these "instructions" did not come very often, but when they did, I followed their guidance to the letter. I told him that I knew this was a lot to ask of a spouse, but Daniel agreed, and we started planning our wedding. Life went on as normal for us in the Smoky Mountains of the Carolinas…

. . .until that fateful day the message came. I was minding my own business when my Spirit Team summoned me loud and clear. Their instructions: *It's time to move back home to Mississippi, where you will now be known as The Mississippi Medium.* Come again? I can't possibly be hearing you correctly. I have an established business in liberal New Age Asheville, my husband simply adores where we live, and you want me to pick up and relocate to the Bible Belt, where there are more churches than in any other state? Not to mention that as a vegan, I was living in a food paradise of plant- based healthy culinary possibilities. In Mississippi, if you can't fry it, and if the food didn't originally belong to an animal, you can't possibly serve it. Many Mississippians even put dead pigs in their green beans for goddess sakes. I thought seriously about pretending I had not heard this message. But then I recalled what a mess my life had been in the past whenever I had not heeded my Spirit Team's suggestions.

Based on past instructions, I knew I must listen to the guidance. I rehearsed how I would break this news to my hippie husband. In the end it went something like this. Me: "How was your day, babe?" Daniel: "Busy, but good. How about your day, Panda?" Daniel's pet name for me is Panda, in case you were wondering why on earth my husband was referring to me as a large round black and white bear. But for me, this term of endearment is the sweetest sound I've ever heard. Me: "Good... Well, the instructions came, babe." Daniel: "What instructions are those?" Me: "Remember how

I told you that sometimes my Spirit Team instructs me to do certain things? Well, my new set of instructions is to move back home to Mississippi." Daniel: "Absolutely not! Not going to happen! My job is here and it's going well. Plus, I consider where we live to be paradise. Why on Earth would I move out of paradise?" I gently, or maybe it wasn't so gently, explained that we *would* be moving to Mississippi, so he should really start getting used to the idea. He continued to resist. I know how the Universe works in such matters, so I compromised with Daniel. I said to him, "Will you agree that if we are meant to move, your job will start changing in some way, and that will be your message and sign?" Daniel agreed to this, and I began making plans to move as I knew the Universe would take care of the rest. About two months later, Daniel's job began to change to the point that he could not be happy staying in it. He was finally ready to let our fate unfold. We made the move to Mississippi a couple of months later.

At this point, we still had no idea of all the intricate details of what our soul contracts involved regarding Mississippi. We were both in deep depression after first arriving. As for me, I was still heavily grieving my mom. I missed all the yummy vegetarian restaurants that we frequented in Asheville. Who would I connect with? Were there any other eccentrics who shared my beliefs here? I don't participate in organized religion, and the very first thing a Southerner asks upon meeting you is, where do you go to church? So, I was not connecting with anyone on that level. And lastly, I thought I was probably the only psychic in the entire state. Until I met Duann.

One day I decided to do an internet search to see if there were any other psychics in Mississippi and I came across professional psychic Duann Kier. I was both shocked and delighted! Wow! There are two of us here! I then found her on Facebook and saw that she had started a group in Mississippi called Metaphysical Mississippi! I was elated. There *were* people like me in Mississippi! I decided to private message Duann and ask if she would be interested in having lunch with me. She wholeheartedly agreed as she had recently seen me on Facebook too and wanted to introduce herself. We both admitted to each other later that we had some nervous energy meeting each other. After all, some psychics were known to be territorial and competitive. But we had an instant connection and felt as if we had known each other forever. Duann explained to me that Mississippi had called her home a few years earlier too, and she had listened to the call. During that lunch date, I told Duann that I still had no clue as to exactly why I had been instructed to return to the Deep South. What Duann explained next made my jaws drop open. She told me that two separate people she knew had received readings from two separate psychics in other states, and the message had been that Mississippi was eventually going to be a New Age Mecca. It was quite shocking to hear this and almost unbelievable, yet I had the goosebumps all over my body, which is one of my ways of validating a knowing. Duann relayed to me that Jackson, Mississippi, was built over a volcano and the energy was intense. Apparently, many others who had moved away over the years had mysteriously been "called" to move back. She excitedly told me that there were now many gifted people living in the Magnolia State and that there was a huge awakening going on. We became instant friends and soul sisters, aware that we had special work to accomplish together.

A few months later, I received the inspiration and guidance that Daniel and I were to open a metaphysical wellness center. The human Jill argued with this revelation, as Mississippi is in the Deep South. There is a church on just about every corner. How could a New Age business even survive, much less thrive, in such a market? However, the "deep knowing" Jill started receiving the downloads and blueprints of what the Center would be like. I decided to call Duann and ask her advice on this undertaking. Duann was excited and told me that I needed to meet Karen Parker, who had previously owned a successful metaphysical store called New Vibrations. I later learned that Karen had truly jumped off that cliff opening her store years earlier, when someone would not have believed there were *any* New Agers hidden in Mississippi. Duann arranged for Karen and me to meet, and Karen agreed to help us get started. Karen Parker and New Vibrations bravely paved the way for the genesis of the New Age Movement in our beautiful state.

It was then that Soul Synergy Center was birthed. I knew I wanted the name Soul in the name. And then Spirit gave me the name Synergy. Synergy means the interaction or cooperation of two or more forces to produce a combined effect greater than the sum of their separate effects. This touched me on a deep level, as I knew this Center was not meant to be just about me or just about one main practitioner, or even just one main modality. I knew this Center was meant to be a nucleus of energetic Light, sending out signals of peace, love, and acceptance of all. A place where people could work from, and share their gifts with others. A place where people in the community could come and enjoy the fellowship of others of like minds. Our mission statement became this: Soul Synergy Center is an energy hub. We celebrate and nurture all aspects of being— mind, body, and spirit—and commune together in pursuit of healing, transformation, and personal connection. We invite you to join us: to escape the stresses of life, energize your full being, expand your awareness, and enjoy the camaraderie of your colleagues and friends.

Daniel and I birthed this Center on a wing and a prayer. It has been the toughest hill we have had to climb, yet the most rewarding thing we have ever done. We now realize that it was in our soul contract to open this amazing healing sanctuary that was so much needed in Mississippi. It still brings tears to my eyes when our customers walk through the door and genuinely thank us for opening a place where they can come to relax and refresh themselves from the stresses of life.

It would be careless of me to talk about birthing my dream of a metaphysical center without acknowledging everyone who did their part in bringing this dream to fruition. First and foremost, my unwavering gratitude goes out to my beloved Daniel, who firmly believed in me and my vision. This Center would not be in existence without Daniel. When you look at this situation from a strictly 3D perspective, we didn't have the funds necessary to pull off such a venture. Daniel agreed to use his entire retirement account to fund this endeavor. And please believe me when I say this fund was not vast by any stretch of the imagination. Yet my husband handed over his life savings to help me realize my dreams. And if this weren't enough of a love offering to me, he signed his name on a mountain of debt. This may be a good time for you to go find a barf bag, because guys, I'm about to get really mushy. Daniel is my real-world knight in shining armor. My love for this man is difficult to put into words. I adore him from the depths of my soul. He is a man who is strong, intelligent, and capable, yet he wears his divine feminine crown with pride.

Duann and Karen met me at every potential location for over six months as we searched for the perfect place. We knew it would not be until each one of us got the full *knowing* that we had found the destined space. We finally did find that place in November of 2017, and immediately started to get everything ready.

My brother-in-law David worked long exhausting hours on top of his full-time job, helping us organize the Center and build our salt cave. My nephew Tyler offered his help as well. Wendy, my sister, graced the Center with her amazing design services. She transformed one of the bathrooms in a way that prompted people to ask who our professional designer was.

My stepson Austin provided one of the necessary loans for the Center! This was a proud mama moment when I knew my son had listened to my guidance while growing up about saving money, and the importance of proper investing. Austin was overjoyed to be able to provide this loan for the Center while receiving interest on his investment at the same time. I was elated that his energy would be connected to the

Center as well!

One day early on in our business, a bill came due that we had no idea how we were going to pay. My human side worried that our perfect credit could be tarnished, yet I prayed and surrendered, asking for Divine help. The next day, my dad texted me, asking if he could stop by the house. Dad walked in and handed me an envelope of cash in the exact amount we needed to pay this debt. He said he had seen Daniel and me and David, Tyler, and Wendy working so hard to bring the Center to life that he wanted to contribute in some way. As Dad drove away, I sobbed. I shed tears of gratitude that I was blessed beyond measure to have chosen the dad I chose. And I cried because I had once again witnessed the magic of the Universe. "Ask and it shall be given to you." I had not asked my dad for this money. I would never have done so. I simply prayed and asked for Divine Guidance, and my dad got the "signal" on the etheric level. My awe is still childlike when I witness the enchantment of this mystical Universe.

When we step onto the path we are meant to navigate, others are proud to walk beside us, impacting us in some way. Remember that there are many ways to offer assistance to others. I thank God every day for those people in my life who have contributed in any way to bringing my dreams to life.

Duann and I had both taught psychic and intuitive

development classes for many years. I got a message that we were to combine our efforts and teach our intuitive development classes together. I asked Duann to meditate on this and see if it resonated for her. She did, and was told by her guides that it was definitely a green light. Mississippi Academy for Spirituality was born out of Soul Synergy. This was truly a dream come true for Duann and me and many other spiritual teachers, who now had a sacred space where they could share their wisdom and gifts with others. As Duann and I completed our first yearlong program together and watched the remarkable transformation in our students, we were both brought to tears.

I talk about Soul Tribes throughout this book. Mississippi has bestowed upon me another one of my Soul Tribes. The tag line Duann created for Metaphysical Mississippi is this: "The more we shine the light on each other, the more enlightened we all become." Feel the deep resonance of these words for a moment. With Metaphysical Mississippi and with Soul Synergy Center we have created an energy and an atmosphere where competition can't survive. Competitive energy is of a lower vibration. An energy or belief in lack, or the idea that there is not enough to go around, lowers the frequency. As we step further into the fifth-dimensional frequency, those who feel more comfortable in the lower frequencies of scarcity will not be able to sustain their energy

ABOUT THE AUTHOR

The Mississippi Medium, Jill M Jackson, is an international award winning highly sought after Psychic Medium and Spiritual Teacher having won such prestigious awards such as the 2016 and 2015 Psychic of the Year from Best American Psychics! She was also awarded the 2014 Social Activism Award from Best American Psychics for her volunteer work with animals.

One of her great passions is being of service as a Spiritual Teacher and helping others ignite, refine, and hone their gifts! Whether you are desiring to deepen your Intuition to help in your career and personal life or whether you feel you have a calling to become a Professional Psychic or Medium, consider allowing Jill to help you navigate your way! Visit www.JillMJackson.com to sign up for Jill's newsletter and to also read about her classes.

Jill lives in Mississippi with her beloved husband Daniel and their four dogs.

Made in the USA
Monee, IL
26 August 2019